AROUND THE WORLD ON EIGHTY PRAYERS

Hilary McDowell, performance poet and author has utilised her skills in drama, poetry and psychology for christian healing and evangelism. Within the ministry of wholeness Hilary has, for the past 21 years, served in the full-time vocation of Deaconess of the Presbyterian Church in Ireland and is much in demand as a speaker throughout the UK and beyond. Her first book, *Some Day I'm Going to Fly*, testifies to God's enablement through a lifetime meeting the challenges of multiple disabilities from birth, against the backdrop of the Ulster troubles. This follow-up selection of stories and poetry from her travels around the world traces afresh the leading of God in all circumstances, and celebrates anew the Christian injunction to trust the Lord in every situation.

*To my sister Dorothy whose wanderlust
is as insatiable as my own*

AROUND THE WORLD ON EIGHTY PRAYERS

Hilary McDowell

TRIANGLE

First published 1997
Triangle
SPCK
Holy Trinity Church
Marylebone Road
London NW1 4DU

Bible quotations are from the Revised Standard Version
of the Bible © 1971 and 1952.

British Library Cataloguing-in-Publication Data
A catalogue record for this book is available from the
British Library.

ISBN 0-281-04919-X

Typeset by Pioneer Associates, Perthshire
Printed and bound in Great Britain by
BPC Paperbacks Ltd.

CONTENTS

POEMS

MALADY OR MELODY

Travelling in the restlessness
Of motivated life,
Malady or melody,
Sweet malaise of passion,
Creativity of strife.
Not discontent or futile,
Yet always moving on.
Where Spirit blows we know not,
Relinquishing the permanence,
To comprehend his call.

PREFACE

The webbed feet scrabbled the surface of the water into a flurry of agitation as it landed, launching its rounded body into a spiral of ripples. The duck was afloat and I was left staring, wondering where it would go. Soon its navigation was confluent in the mix of a dozen other species of wildfowl, all flapping, preening and pecking their way around the man-made haven of tall reed beds and carefully appointed islands.

Castle Espie, outside the village of Comber in Northern Ireland, is a most beautiful place where tall trees and meticulously kept lawns host migrant fowl from as far as Iceland, Africa, and Australia.

The smew, the teal, the brent-geese, make phenomenal journeys for a winter sanctuary among the reflections of these integrally landscaped little pools and bridges. How I love the peace of the place, undisturbed by the cackle and caw of the inhabitants. Each swan-trumpet a salve to human ears which have been conditioned by car-horns and raucous telephone jangle.

But where was he going, that duck? To eat, to sleep, to establish himself in the variable pecking order of the flock? I so wanted to converse with him. Would he be too busy pursuing his next conquest, or fishing for his next meal, to delight me with tales of the journey from the Arctic?

Had he noticed how the ice-peaks of the mountains spread below his wings were sometimes indistinguishable from the chill clouds through which he battled towards the warm? Indistinguishable until the sun's emerging pale touch threw the shadow of his full-stretched span against the snow. Did he know how beautiful were his feathers then, illuminated in the light, unaware of the envy of eagles as he flew?

Maybe he did understand. Who are we, pompous humanity, to assume that only intelligence arranged in human mode can comprehend the whisperings of scenic grandeur, the invisible miracle of divine guidance, the depth-charge nature of unconditional love?

Perhaps my small bird understands more fully than us the tenet to glorify God and enjoy him forever. See how the duck traverses continents without frontiers, needing neither passport nor insurance to oil his passage nor bolster his confidence.

For me, the seeking of the earth in place and beauty, in culture and experience, has always been a rough road – and spectacular. I travel, not to arrive, but to know that the journey is worthwhile. At pre-school age, when asked what I wanted to do when I grew up, I replied, 'To see the world and tell people about God'. Seeing is indeed believing, for God goes with me and walks before me all the way. A belief in him has made all my travels possible.

This book is not a catalogue of the journey. It is no blow-by-blow account of stations reached. I was no Phileas Fogg competing against the clock to cover some prearranged itinerary. Instead I just went exploring in full expectation of pleasure and pain, carrying with me the hardest burden of all – myself.

Physically equipped or not, wise or not, I had to come along for the ride. There didn't seem to be an alternative at the time; there never is. We take ourselves, or we do not go. There is no other option open to the human condition.

The motivator of my pilgrimage is also my companion. Without the Lord I could not take another step nor breathe another breath. Communication with him has been both my compass and my strength.

The road lies ahead. May we travel a distance together, exploring the sensations, trials, gifts and surprises of visiting many places around the earth on eighty prayers?

1 THREE WHEELS ON MY WAGON

Scotland: The Cuillins on Skye –
Mull and Iona – Glencoe

I knew it was coming. I'd been interviewed for it, examined for it, measured, prepared and programmed for it. Its necessity was well accepted, and I acknowledged its practicability within my mind. My spirit was struggling to be sensible. Like all good souls it was talking sternly to itself about needs and necessities, advantages and potential.

If this was the case, why was the first sight of a brand-new, shining, invalid car parked outside my front door sufficient to produce one of the most intensely sharp pains I had ever experienced? Broken pride, devastating in all its teenage poignancy, could not have proved more hurtful. That little innocent blue blob at my front door was saying something I had never consciously said to myself: 'You are disabled.'

It wasn't just saying it, it was advertising the fact in a blazoned manner; and not just to me, but to the neighbours, to strangers, to careless passers-by, to everyone. As if written in letters a mile high and wide on the gable of our wall the legend proclaimed for all to see, 'Here liveth a disabled person'. Only not 'liveth' any longer. That day I felt something vital had died in me – the part of Hilary which stood erect and firm, head high and spirit bright. I felt that the invisible legend now bore the words, 'Here dwelleth a disabled person'.

The arrival of the car taught me nothing I did not already know. Owning multiple disabilities from birth, I knew that I was handicapped and so did everyone else, but those disabilities had never prevented me from practising a complete and hectic life-style. God had enabled me to participate fully in everyday society. But what hurt now was the fear that folk would somehow imagine that I had thrown in the towel. It is one thing to be disabled, and to know it and accept it and have no reason to apologise for it, while at the same time being determined to accept also the challenge of living as fully as possible a 'normal' life (whatever normal is, exactly!) It is quite another thing to be disabled, and to know it and accept it and, at the same time, accept an instrument of a life marked 'not normal'. An instrument that might brand me 'refuser of the challenge' for ever. This was my rather immature thinking at that time. To me, in those early days, the three-wheeler seemed to be just such an instrument, bless him. But right then, blessing him I was not. I had never refused a challenge in my life, so how could I possibly accept his presence outside my door?

All who have suffered similar indignities, in various shapes and forms, know that it takes time to adjust, a great deal of time; and every moment of that time the hurt plays continual discords in the back of your mind through good days and bad, through progress and stalemate. But a teenager, no matter how she may feel to the contrary, is never truly at stalemate. Moving on is obligatory in life, and maturity is usually time's gradual reward for surviving its passing. During our first year together the little blue trike and I survived each other's attentions. It took us much longer to fall in love.

How did you learn to drive? Did you suffer at the hands of a loving relative, thus risking family unity and domestic bliss? Did you throw caution to the wind and persuade a collection of friends to go out on a run with you, against their better judgement? Or did you trust one of the professional motoring schools which guarantees satisfaction or your money back?

Whichever choice you made, you had a choice. Not so for the would-be driver of an invalid car during my teenage years. Nowadays excellent instruction and computer simulation is available for the disabled learner-driver. But at that time the only way to learn was to get on the road, solo.

It was illegal to carry passengers; besides which, there was no room and relatives could drive a trike no better than the learner. The statutory lessons from the approved instructor were restricted to his pointing out the dials, throttle, gear-stick and brake-lever with his head stuck through the door. He attempted to address my questions and ended with a cheery smile and a wave as he left with the famous last words: 'There you are, luv, you're on your own – there's nothing to it.'

The two lessons amounted to three hours in total and, although I had been blessed with an excellent and patient instructor, it was with great trepidation that I set off for the lonely six months probationary period before the test.

I suppose it is not too surprising that my only serious accident in an invalid car took place during this period of 'learning the hard way'. It happened as I was attempting to turn right out of a side street into a four-lane main road. The traffic in the inside lane stopped to allow me to turn out, the kind driver in front of the stationary traffic signalled me to pull out round him – but with disastrous results. I had failed to realise what every experienced driver knows: that cars in the outside lane, blocked from view, had no awareness of me, and in this instance, no intention of stopping despite the fact that they might have wondered why the inner lane had stopped. So, thanks to my inexperience and the other driver's careless speed, I found myself, not only in full collision, but with my car's front nose cleanly chopped off only inches away from my feet. It was a miracle I still had legs, for a fibreglass body is no protection against a collision. It was also a blessing that my fellow victim was not injured, for the impact was at speed. He was greatly relieved to discover that my stature was normally 4 feet 6 inches (1.37m), and I had not lost my legs in his impromptu amputation of the trike's elongated nose.

I too was pleased to discover that invalid cars could receive fibreglass transplants which enabled large sections of their body to be replaced and welded on. Thus it was that my poor steed, only weeks after birth, was relegated to a patched up 'half-caste' with a two-shaded exterior. Fibreglass he may have continued to be on the outside, but from that day on the little blue blob began to develop a personality all his own. Maybe, somehow, the accident had made us even. Maybe some of my resentment towards him had been dissipated. Perhaps, having suffered together, we could now learn to live together, or maybe, just maybe, he was now bearing the scars for me. Whatever the reason, we had been properly introduced and the hatchet was buried.

A personality in his own right must have a name. A machine is a machine. But suffering builds character and a machine that suffers earns a personality. He may have started life as a thorn in my flesh, but St Paul had coped pretty well with thorns in the flesh and, in God's strength, there was no reason why I couldn't live with mine, drive with mine, share some adventures with mine. So this little piece of mechanised transport, this three-wheeled wagon, I duly christened Hullrontebib (Bib for short) – an anagram of 'Blue Thorn Lib', acknowledging its colour, its painful associations, and the liberation potential it promised in terms of physical independence.

Having driven to destruction in two easy lessons, our next big hurdle was the test. There was no room for an examiner beside the driver, no heavy breathing down my neck. Good, you might think, much to be preferred – or is it? At least when he is in beside you, you know where he is and what is happening (well, most of the time). Instead, everything had to be done by remote control. The instructor stood on the pavement, explained what he wanted me to do, sent me off alone, and kept popping up all around the block at intervals to watch, from outside, how I was doing it. Disconcerting for most exercises, but let me tell you about the emergency stop.

It sounded quite straightforward. The instructor explained: 'Just drive around again, keep going at a constant speed of thirty miles per hour, and at my own discretion I'll step out of a hidden doorway and throw a cushion into the centre of the road in front of you.' The idea was to stop suddenly, making sure that the cushion was not touched. It sounds reasonable enough, doesn't it? Indeed it does, and I stopped, believe me I stopped. Only it wasn't a cushion.

In front of my wheels in the middle of the road sprawled a full grown male personage who, having thrown himself full-length and at speed in front of my oncoming wheels, picked himself up, dusted himself down, wandered in an unconcerned manner towards my open door where my shattered nerves were trying to reassemble themselves, and grinned cheerily. 'Sorry,' he said, 'I couldn't find a cushion.' I passed my test.

Take a wagon, any wagon, lose a wheel and what have you got? Answer: a bumpy ride. But even a bumpy ride can be enjoyable if you're getting somewhere. But that was the trouble; I wasn't.

The fact that an invalid car is only supposed to have three wheels is not much comfort when you find yourself in the middle of the Cuillins. These high mountains on the Isle of Skye proved a challenge for Bib. I am afraid I wasn't out of petrol, nor did the points need cleaning. I considered the possibility that the engine had just overheated and needed time to cool down. It was a good guess and lines along which the Sherlock Holmes of the motor trade might well have progressed had he been there – but he wasn't, I was. Since I was there I could not ignore that loud and most ominous thud from behind, the one that had preceded my chariot grinding to a halt.

When you are alone, stuck, on a tiny one-track sheep-trail, in the middle of the Cuillins, in an invalid car, and such a thud has come from behind, where the engine normally resides, it takes a little courage to climb out and look back. But if I was to have my worst fears confirmed, then it might as well be before darkness fell over the mountains.

Sure enough, an inspection of the back of the car

revealed nothing. That's the trouble – it should have revealed the engine but, on opening the lid, I discovered only a large space where an engine used to be and a few yards behind there lay, in the middle of the road, one two-stroke engine, fully intact, and probably in working order, except that it was parted from its cocoon. I was no mechanic, but even I knew that an engine without a body is indeed a poor means of transport.

I stared at the offending broken undershaft which, before it snapped, had been the only thing between my throbbing components and the road beneath, and slightly regretted my attempt to drive all the way round Skye in half a day. Not that such a journey is beyond the realms of possibility, even for an invalid car, but considering that the trip came in the middle of a 1,000-mile circuit of youth hostels in Scotland – well, it had been quite a week for the wee car, and I hadn't exactly chosen the most gentle route for my steed. If you want to see the sights from Edinburgh, to Aberdeen, to Inverness, to Skye you have got to climb a few hills, if you will pardon the understatement.

At that precise moment, being 15 miles from the nearest hamlet, I might as well have been in the most uncivilised place in the world. Come to think of it, the Isle of Skye is not exactly Piccadilly Circus. I waited. There is nothing else a disabled driver can do in such circumstances, except wait.

Supposing it had happened in Edinburgh, I thought: there are people there, walking by, driving past. A nearby sheep sauntered up to my bonnet and bleated contemptuously. I mused that it was strange how the hills looked more threatening than they had done a few moments previously. Was that a sound? I twisted round in my seat to scan the road stretching up through the misty grey peaks of the Cuillins. I hadn't noticed the mist before. That sound came again, the gentle muttering of a nearby stream. Its liquid coldness made me shiver. I wondered how far the temperature would drop when darkness fell. Hey, I thought, don't be ridiculous, Hilary, there is no reason why you should have to sit here all night. Only there was a reason. As I said, the Isle of Skye is no Piccadilly Circus.

It hadn't occurred to me to pray. My whole journey so far had been a prayer. Every bump, every corner, every unknown highway, and sometimes, when you do something for a long time in an unbroken attitude of prayer, it seems ludicrous to pray formally. I had planned the journey in the presence of God. I had cherished the expectation of it in the presence of God. I'd prepared for it, packed for it, propelled myself into it, in the presence of God, and now, in his presence, I was stuck. I wondered what he had up his sleeve this time. In my short experience of life many things have failed me, many have disappointed, but never, at any time have I ceased to wonder at God's perfect timing and, above all, his sense of humour.

Amidst sheep and bracken I don't know what I expected to see, but there, coming out of a ramshackle wee lean-to hut, about a hundred yards across the bog, appeared a shepherd. An elderly soul who had probably spent most of his life quietly tending his animals and keeping out of the curious glances of tourists. I deduced that he would most certainly never have set eyes on a three-wheeled, government-supplied invalid tricycle. He strolled over and surveyed the scene in a most unconcerned manner. I smiled nervously and he nodded politely. I was attempting not to feel as though I had just materialised before him in Doctor Who's Tardis – but when he enquired, 'What seems to be the trouble?' I found it extremely difficult to use a solemn tone as I replied, 'I think my engine's fallen out.'

Incredible though it seems, there was no hint of either amazement or amusement in his voice as he walked to the rear of the car muttering, 'I'll sort it for you.' 'What's he going to use?' I wondered. 'Magic?' But in all my careful calculations of Skye, I had not reckoned on the jack-of-all-trades nature of its inhabitants. Having hitched the engine back into its original position, resting precariously between the broken ends of the shaft which had once held it secure, my new friend proceeded to haul from the hut coils of wire which looked to me, a novice in such matters, to be of the type used for making sheep-fences. Then he dexterously wound it around and through and in and out of the engine and its surround, until the spider's web was complete and the machine was securely held fast within its tangle.

'There you are,' announced my rescuer. 'That will take you the 15 miles to Broadford.' Such faith, I thought to myself – but thanked him profusely and managed not to look surprised as my turning the key in the ignition resulted in an immediate and healthy purring of the reinstated engine.

Fifteen miles is an awfully long way when every little bump and jolt in the road threatens to de-engine you again. But we made it. Broadford had everything a tourist might expect to find in a small town on Skye: school, cottages, all the usual quaint Scottish-type items in the shops, the local pub (but not for a life-long teetotaller like me). This tourist, grateful though she was to have arrived somewhere which boasted a garage, none the less did not expect the mechanics to be able to repair an invalid trike any more than they could be expected to repair a passing flying-saucer. Indeed it was my experience that, except for the very minor ailments (into which category a severed engine did not come) the necessary help could only be found at the local, official, government-approved, government-trained repair garage for invalid cars. Unfortunately such places tended to be situated in large cities and were few and far between. I shivered to consider the consequences of a hundred or more mile trek to a suitably qualified 'trike Doc'.

I suppose I should have known better by now. Thinking logically is an extremely useful mental exercise but it seldom allows for the kind of coincidence which recurs so often throughout my life as to make it unbelievable, were it not proven by my experience that fact is indeed stranger than fiction.

Close to Broadford, a disabled driver had, some time previous to my visit, pointed out to the Ministry the difficulty, not to mention expense, of transporting his vehicle the long distance to the nearest official mainland servicing station for frequent repair. One of the Broadford mechanics had recently been trained and fully authorised to carry out maintenance and repair work, thus ensuring that the necessary service was available right on the driver's doorstep. My car was expertly made new again and restored to me with the mechanic's firm assurance of its roadworthiness. Not the end of the trip after all, I thought – and indeed the best was still to come.

Mull is a wee gem of an island, satisfying as it does my lust for barren beauty, for gentle blue hills and always and forever the sweet, unmitigated tang of the sea, never out of reach, only occasionally out of view. Such variety of beauty changes each moment as you drive. Its name sounds unromantic, its history overshadowed by many lesser rocks, but it is by far the most beautiful small island I have ever experienced. I drove across it with joy singing in my heart and the expectation of Iona still to come.

Iona is smaller still and although it has not Mull's beauty, to it belongs the history and reverence of centuries of saintly inhabitants. So often had I listened painfully to enthusiastic tourists with harsh, penetrating voices, raving at great length about the 'atmosphere' and 'aura' of Iona that, with a stubborn and objective eye, I was determined to relegate all such effluence to the realm of emotional wishful thinking on the part of soul-weary tourists from bustling urban human zoos. But I was in for a lesson worth learning. I won't try to convince you that there is a peace resting within the rocks and waves and scraggy grass of Iona which exceeds the normal logical explanation of absence of noise, and rat-race and 'civilisation'. There just is, that's all. Believe me, take me at my word, or better still, go yourself and discover; but either way, please do not imagine it to be an ordinary lump of rock in the middle of the sea.

After the relaxing drive across Mull I steered confidently down the rough stones to a pier which was accustomed to hold only feet, not wheels. Low over the water the slight wooden planks groaned as the three-wheeled car drove onwards towards the splashing waves.

I had a lovely feeling of wanting to drive on in and enjoy the splash, but disciplined the urge and applied the brakes. The queue of onlookers patiently awaiting the return of the tiny ferry to take them to Iona were too polite to say what they thought of my sanity – but their glances were communicative enough.

Naturally, I had exchanged much correspondence with the ferry company long before I arrived to attempt such a crossing. Nowadays a car ferry does this job most efficiently, but in the mid-1970s no such luxury existed. I had been assured that such a transaction was by no means impossible and had been successfully attempted over the years with the doctor's car, the Abbey car, and a small assortment of necessary farm implements and machinery – but, from the expressions on the faces of the boatmen, I could tell that this was no everyday commission.

Hullrontebib was not large, not heavy and not wide – that is if you compare him with four-wheeled cars. However, if you compare his proportions with the size of an eleven-foot-wide motor boat, things might appear to be less matter-of-fact than at first imagined. Add to this the fact that the ferryman had decided to lay the two separate planks (which were to be Hullrontebib's supports) widthways across, not lengthways along, the boat, and you may begin to understand how my heart missed a few beats as I attempted to board. The planks were laid wide enough to support the back wheels while the front wheel 'walked the tightrope' of a raised section of the boat. I looked at these planks extending a good few inches over either side of the craft and felt the hair at the back of my neck rising as the goosepimples pricked my skin. Alongside the little pier the boat bobbed jocularly up and down, allowing the planks several hair-raising inches of movement above the landing-stage. To ride safely on to them I knew I must accelerate to a degree which threatened to force me to overshoot the other side of the boat and instantly turn poor Bib into an 'amphicar'! I became less anxious to experience that splash of freedom as it became more probable.

Until now I had never fully appreciated the extent to which a motor-boat can tilt and dip on a rough crossing. How the car didn't just slide into the sea during one of the swells is beyond my comprehension. The incredible tilt of the wee vehicle and the fact that nothing but his own brakes stood between him and a watery grave, made the exercise anything but tranquil. I actually managed to get out of the car during the crossing – a feat in itself – and sat wondering if I might bid my belongings farewell at any moment. But arrive safely we did, despite my fears, and I unloaded the vehicle to the strain of the ferryman's voice informing me, in an unconcerned manner, that there was no guarantee he could get me back again at the end of the week – 'It depends', he said, 'on the weather.'

You too must have memories that make you shiver slightly in the recall. And shivering makes you think that someone has just walked over your grave – and maybe they did, or maybe the memory did, for grave-walking memories are all too sure a part of life, and perhaps exist to make the sun look a little brighter when it shines, or love feel a little warmer, or life that much more precious.

Scenery is not all gentle and beautiful: often it is rugged, and still more beautiful. Maybe it's something gone wrong in my interior suspension that makes me yearn for the sea in its hurtling, swirling, spray-flinging rage, or mountains that overshadow, overpower, overbear, in jagged, pinnacled, uncompromising awesomeness. There is a fertile response within me that makes itself felt most acutely in the midst of barren splendour.

Glencoe *is* history, its steep mountain-sides sweeping towards heaven while hell-bent memories of massacres cower in its valley. Most tourists drive delightfully through it, enjoying the grandeur and sipping history pleasantly with mid-morning coffee-stops and afternoon teacups, and buy a postcard for Auntie Mildred on the way, but not me.

As Hullrontebib had learned to his cost, I'm not a tourist, I'm a traveller. But that is no excuse, no excuse at all, for having driven him to near-destruction all week. I was desperate to get to the nearest youth hostel before dark. It is 9.30 on a dark night in March, and the car's steaming and spluttering and backfiring at a maximum of 30 mph because it has been over-heating all day, and there hasn't been a house for ten miles and there won't be another for the next twenty, and the overbearing mountains aren't doing much to help, and the valley's morbid history isn't doing much to help, and my state of physical and mental exhaustion isn't doing much to help, and even if we gave up the ghost only one mile from help, wherever that might be, it would still be one mile too far for a disabled driver, in a three-wheeled wagon, in dead of night, in Glencoe.

Speed is now ten miles an hour maximum. Bib's not limping any more, he's dragging himself along on all-threes. There is no longer any sensation of movement – just the deafening noise of a none the less feeble two-stroke engine in my ears. What was that in the glare of the headlamps? A wee mouse? A rabbit?

14

Yes, both – and more: foxes, rodents, hares; animals, lots of animals.

The crawling beam of my headlight along its narrow pointed way picked up a continual procession of small wildlife. Had I stopped? It felt like it, but no, like a snake on its belly Bib gripped the tarmac and pulled himself agonisingly onward.

The headlamps went dim momentarily. Were they fading? No. Then it happened again. They weren't fading, their light was being blocked, fleetingly by something – but what? Already totally fraught, my nerve-ends could only just manage a last desperate quiver as the awful grace of its wet beating wings framed itself in my headlights, and clung for seconds across my front windscreen. Was its name 'bat' or was it much larger, as it seemed? But in the darkness, who can assess, who knows? I only know it appeared to be monstrous. I gasped a prayer to my master. For what seemed like moments it blacked the window and then was gone. God be thanked for its departure, whatever it was.

I did not pray to Bib, I urged him, in the name of the one to whom I do pray, to get me home. Oh, please, please, I lent my whole body, mind and soul to the willing of it, and on Bib clawed his way. Can a machine do more than is possible for machinery to do? Can nuts, bolts and carburettor perform beyond what is deemed mechanically possible? Can technology be baffled, confounded and totally dumbfounded at, dare I say, a miracle? That can sometimes be a dirty word in the world of nuts and bolts, but all I know is that a little piece of machinery, loved and cared for, though not well enough I know, and granted a char-acter all its own through many deeds and misdeeds can, in the hands of God, become for just a short moment of a night, something capable of an incredible rescue from the Valley of . . .

Hullrontebib breathed his last and irrevocably stopped – dead. Where? Exactly three feet from the door of a building which bore the legend 'Youth Hostel'.

Partings are supposed to be emotional – at least they are in all the best movies. But this was no movie, I wasn't an American starlet and Bib was no hero in shining armour. Just a wee blue, slightly battered, much scarred invalid car of the ripe old age of seven, who was being turned out to graze.

I suppose I should have felt guilty, waving good-bye to a trusty steed who had borne me over countless miles of tears and joy. But to see me standing beside a large, blue, shining four-wheeled Daf automatic, hand-controlled car, with a brand-new driving licence giving me a legal right to a 'normal' slice of road and the rightful luxury of carrying passengers, I knew, gave Bib almost as much pleasure as it afforded me.

So there were no tears as I handed over his keys outside the City Hall in Belfast and watched the government mechanic unceremoniously hop inside and drive him away. Not a bitter-sweet parting at all – just the expected transaction when an invalid car was no longer young enough, or needed enough, to continue in use. He would be semi-retired to the lighter work of transporting mechanics back and forward on their errands of mercy to broken-down invalid cars, or lent out now and again as a spare. Quite a routine end for a government trike. There was nothing dramatic about the parting and no lumps in the throat. Just an awfully queer feeling of loss, and a weird emptiness somewhere in the region of the stomach.

I whispered a little prayer (not heresy, I'm sure), thanksgiving for a small hunk of machinery that had lived and breathed and moved upon the face of the earth in human fashion. A word of gratitude to the maker of all things for what had been learnt, the hard way.

I waved to Bib's retreating back window. If he could, I think he would have waved back, but he was intent on keeping his present driver on the road. Into the distance I watched him go with no tears, feeling only gratitude and the warmth of memories – and could it be, *could* it be, love?

GROWING UP

Each to each the same ambition,
Chrysalis to butterfly,
River spawn to frog,
Who knows how high the price will be?
The high cost of maturity?
Who sees the dragon insect fly?
This one day free, and same day die?
Who saw the child in feeding trough?
Did wise men recognise a king?
Shepherd boy a lamb?
One knows how high the cost will be,
The high cost of maturity,
See who from crib to cross was led.
And in our growing share his bed.

2 BRAVE NEW WORLD

New York State – The Big Apple –
Canada

Summer 1974, sandwiched as it was between my two years of Deaconess training at St Colm's College in Edinburgh, presented me with real challenge. When the staff at College announced the details of an English Speaking Union project, taking on two students from every college in Edinburgh for a summer project in America, well, the dreaming began. Each applicant had to write an essay for the initial selection procedure. Helen, another St Colm's student who was in my year and a good friend, also showed great interest in applying and, although we both knew we might not be sent to the same area (even if we were selected), nevertheless we both wrote our essays and sent them off with much prayer.

When I thought of going across the pond to teach in a summer school and work with drug addicts on a rehabilitation programme in the evenings, a rock-fall of fears threatened to bury me. What about the immense heat? What about the walking – how could I get around without a car? What about the mosquitoes? What about . . . ?

When we heard that we had both been short-listed, and then finally accepted, I reminded myself what the Bible says: 'Is anything too hard for God?' (Gen. 18.14).

Prestwick was a much more gracious airport than most, with an air of civility and unhurriedness about it. Take-off was at 5.50 p.m. and we had clear sunshine the whole way, with ever-changing cloud shapes for company, ensuring that there was no time for boredom. Flying over Greenland I could see the ice-mountains shimmering in unshaded sunlight, and more great lumps of glistening snow in the azure sea as icebergs seemed, at this vast distance of 35,000 feet, to nudge each other like playful whales because of the kinetic illusion produced by the plane's motion.

Montreal lay below us in all its dignity, and the Hudson River was clearly visible – a ribbon of guidance tracing the pathway to our destination. But I was completely unprepared for the excitement of touchdown. Descent into New York literally took my breath away.

My first sight of habitation was a long strip of populated land by the sea and separated almost completely by the river. Then skyscrapers, just a few, came into sight. I had expected to see hundreds, but then this was not downtown New York, not yet. Then came speed-boats on the river, and houses, and then a great many more houses. But I had never expected the dwellings to be so huge, and such large distances apart, and every one surrounded by what seemed to me to be veritable forests of trees. In reality these were only the gardens – but I was not prepared for such luxury and spaciousness and greenery. This is America, I told myself, and suddenly an excitement I had not experienced since I was a child rushed through my veins – the sick-to-the-stomach variety in head and artery, till the stimulation and adrenalin threatened to overwhelm. We were descending steeply now and I supposed that the altitude change and blood-pressure adjustment probably contributed to the sensation. Gripping the arms of my seat, I prayed for control.

We landed at John F. Kennedy Airport at 1.30 a.m. UK-time – but it was 8.30 p.m. in New York and the temperature was 90 degrees in the shade.

Helen and I said our goodbyes, as we had been allocated to projects in different states, and I w herded into the coach bound for Troy in New State, near Albany (the state capital), and abou. 150 miles north of New York City.

The first hour was fantastic, watching strange and unbelievable sights go rushing by, and all seen through a haze of exhaustion and drowsiness. The sheer size of everything eclipsed all else in my sleepy mind. The houses were big, the roads were big, the cars were huge, and the scenery whizzing past seemed to stretch as far as the eye could see on every side.

Darkness fell and it got cold, very cold indeed. After the intense heat on landing, the sudden chill gnawed into my bones. We had pleaded with the driver to switch on the air-conditioning, but now we seriously regretted our request because it remained on regardless of the changing temperature outside and, on arrival at our destination at 11.30 p.m. (5.30 a.m. UK-time), out tumbled an iced leprechaun, shivering to the teeth. I imagined the angels chuckling when I thought of the many fervent prayers I had sent to heaven that my first hours in America would not be too hot so that I would have time to acclimatise.

THINK BEFORE YOU PRAY

Be careful what you pray for,
The angels are all ears,
To accommodate your needs
And allay your every fear,
Be it great or small,
High or low,
Human or divine,
That pious pittance of petition
Travels transfer charges –
Direct line.
Be careful what you pray for,
'Cause I can plainly see,
Everything I've needed
Has come home to roost for me.
So don't be bashful, timid or demure,
A prayer is never something to regret,
Just give some thought to supplication
As you humbly kneel to speak
Remember, what you ask for,
You might get!

The first few days flew by in a haze of jet-lag. Everywhere the surroundings were alien to me, but stimulating. I had to make a mental adjustment to large wooden houses with three floors and sixteen rooms; be introduced to teabags, and hamburgers cooked barbecue-style in the open air; not to mention shopping in a mall which could have housed a small hospital in its main thoroughfare. There were surprises for me: the clothes were more expensive and yet cars and houses much cheaper than I would have imagined, in comparison to home.

Church anywhere in the world always feels like

home to me, but it was interesting to see the small differences in practice. Like the baptism service – my first experience of the minister carrying the baby through the congregation, allowing the children to touch the new-born infant, and sometimes even to hold it, as the service progressed. At that time, in my second week, I was attending another church, when three-year-old Jessie burst into the body of the church from an adjoining door which led to the manse, yelling at his father, who was preaching in pulpit at the time: 'Come quick, Dad. There's a big spill in the kitchen!' If worship is meant to help us get our priorities right, then the smiles on the faces of the congregation was testimony that, on this occasion, it had certainly worked. Pot-luck suppers were held after Sunday evening service, with each member of the congregation contributing from the bounty, or famine, of their week.

On the Monday we were each taken by our respective hosts to begin our work in the South End Day Camp in Troy. It was situated on the site of the local community college, which held as many as 600 pupils in all, including able-bodied, physically disabled, and mentally handicapped children. A good mix for any kind of education and, for a summer school, it was perfect. Great for the kids that is. The teachers, on the other hand, had to have the ingenuity of Einstein and the stamina of Samson.

Before I started I remember being asked what I would like to teach. 'Is there a choice?' I queried, rather pleased to be offered one. 'Yeah,' I was told. 'You can either take Red Indian folklore, or arts and crafts.' You will not be surprised to learn that I chose arts and crafts.

The Red Indian folklore was covered most adequately by Tom Two Arrows, an Indian of one hundred per cent authenticity, who tours the world with his wife promoting their culture; the displays around the camp fire which ended the summer school will live forever in my memory.

Because I was doing arts and crafts, I was not restricted to one of the groups of 15–22 children, but during the course of the camp, all 600 pupils passed at some time through our classroom. This gave a tremendous opportunity to integrate all the disabilities and talents, and to watch folk reach their full potential in the stimulating and ever-changing mix of personality and ability.

The days were challenging and exhausting. As the heat began to climb in the non-air-conditioned building, I was grateful how unquestioningly the children had accepted me. Most of them had heard very little of Ireland and referred to us all as Scots, but they were fascinated by my accent and they knew about leprechauns. I thanked God for my short stature as it proved a real bridge to their friendship and their sense of humour.

I worked with Lloyd, a permanent member of the staff and a teacher of many subjects; we made everything from cork mats to tomahawks, from thermometer-holders, to the children's own esoteric inventions. One of the favourite craft ideas was to make *Ojos de Dios*, meaning 'God's eyes'. The children had loved making these in previous years and insisted on teaching me how. They are a kind of woven cross within a square, and in Mexico are believed to ward off evil spirits. It gave me the opportunity to explain to the children how the one true

God is in control and not any spirit of evil, although we must choose to do God's will and make Jesus our Master, if evil is to be vanquished. I was surprised that there was a great deal of superstition around despite the grossly materialistic, and seemingly sophisticated, culture. In the making and using of puppets I discovered more of the latent drama instincts which would later become a major part of my ministry.

At the weekends the counsellors (of which I was one) were allowed an outing to see something of America. I will never forget our trip to Saratoga National Park. It included a picnic in the park and a wonderful evening at the ballet in the huge outdoor stadium. The Saratoga Hills are beautiful, and straight out of the history books with their famous Indian Snake Ladder Trail.

On another day we visited Thacher Park for a full day's spectacular barbecue picnic. It was a densely wooded area and the humidity was very high. I remember struggling through long grass and at one point feeling a slight tickle on my leg, but, as it was only a tickle, and I was wearing trousers, and trying to keep up with the others, I did not stop to check what it was.

It was not until the next morning that I noticed the swollen and still rising bump on my leg. Already I had hosted quite a number of mosquitoes to a right royal dinner of Ulster blood. They seemed to enjoy the heady mixture, and I had ended up pocked all over like a measles victim – but this one was different. This was the great grand-daddy of all bites. Soon it was evident that it would become the size of a small egg.

As I was speaking to an audience that day, sharing

my insights from Ireland, I tried to ignore the swelling and hoped to do something about it when I had fulfilled my commitments. But the next day, my bite burst and I could see danger-signs in the way it was behaving. That evening I was working in Hope House, the rehabilitation centre for drug addiction in Troy, and the following day we accompanied the children from school on a full day's trip to Grafton, a lovely lakeside park about an hour away. It was teatime before my hostess and I were able to go together for an appointment with her family doctor.

He showed me a large chart on his wall which displayed everything from an ant to a tarantula. I was not too enamoured of the several enormous creatures which (he suggested) might have been responsible for my damaged leg. I left armed with penicillin and ointment to counter the infection – but I was in for a real battle.

At that time I was not aware that I was allergic to penicillin, and in the following days fought staunchly to combat its negative effects. Believing myself merely to be a victim of heat exhaustion, I soldiered on to the end of the project without a break in my work or schedule. Only when I returned home and sought further treatment was I able to recover fully. However, God gave me grace to continue all that he asked me to attempt across the pond.

That night, I was transferred to my second set of lodgings, this time my hostess was a lady minister in an apartment. This friend really knew how to make the most of every moment of the day. She showed me America: drive-in movies, concerts, all-night shopping, a porpoise show, and a John Denver live spectacular in the open air until 3 a.m.

Peggy was a tremendous cook and an accomplished

photographer, and had travelled extensively, taking pictures around the world. One evening, while enjoying her slides of flora and fauna, she commented that a particular picture had puzzled her. It had been taken in the UK and showed a field of bright yellow flowers. She asked if I could identify them as they did not appear in any of her botanical manuals. I stared and stared with wonder at the distance-shot of what looked like a carpet of ripe sunshine. A glorious sight indeed, but I too was puzzled.

We both agreed that the field appeared to be covered by very beautiful flowers – but if only we could see the individual blooms more closely. After much searching, a close-up shot was found of this tiny but resplendent flower, and as it flashed onto the screen I did not know whether to laugh or be silent. For there, quite clearly, in all its brightness, was a close-up of a dandelion. No wonder it was absent from the flower manuals, for ignorant humankind calls this little iridescent glow a weed, and a weed by any other name . . . ?

COMMON AS . . .

Common as unbottled sunshine
As diamonds on wave crest,
Vulgar as leaf tip,
Labelled as weed.
Familiar as sunset
Flame bright in cloud burst,
Deadlocked in mud,
Contempt for its seed.
Victim of slander
Justice withheld,
Foot tramped, beheaded,

Ripped from its bed.
What is the charge now?
Who is the foe?
Gardeners' scourge,
Its offence is to grow.
Spade it and mow it,
Watch lustre die,
Futile, pursue it,
See its wings fly!

Dear Creator,
Who says where the weeds are in your hierarchy
of creation? Who designates flower and weed?
Who appoints which to live and which to die?
Your ways are not our ways. Your values are,
thankfully, not those of a sordid earth whose
estimation of people, as much as things, is based
on their usefulness to humankind's petty agendas
and selfish motivations.

Forgive us Lord, when we fail to appreciate
the brightness of a small created wonder – plant,
man, or beast – merely because we have already
labelled it 'weed'.   *Amen*.

In the final week of the English Speaking Union
Project we were permitted several days free to be
tourists in America – and what a week that was! I
arose at 5 on the first morning and a group of us set
off for the Big Apple. The train travelled along the
banks of the Hudson River to New York.

Then it was Grand Central Station with constant
taped warnings in our ears telling us, 'Hold on to
your belongings', and posters everywhere proclaiming,
'Pickpockets at work'. Then there was the United
Nations Building, with corridors that seemed to be

27

miles long and flags of every country imaginable fanning our every step from above; Wall Street, Trinity Church, Battery Park, Lower Manhattan, the Chrysler Building, City Hall, Greenwich Village, and the Empire State Building with lifts that threatened nose-bleeds because of their incredible speed – and still those inevitable tape-recorded warnings of pickpockets.

On to Times Square and Broadway and the dizzy excitement of a zillion neon lights, one of them announcing the news that President Nixon would fight to stay in office. I watched the rolling words, hypnotised. Brooklyn, to Prospect Heights, viewing Arches at Grand Army Plaza, not to mention the Metropolitan Museum, Fifth Avenue, St Patrick's Cathedral and The Rockefeller Center. It was only for two days, but it felt like a lifetime. How I stood the pace I can only guess. I guess (as the Americans say), that it was by God's grace alone. At times the others had to half-trail, half-carry me along. I was totally exhausted with the heat and the tortuous pace, and my attempt to fight the insect infection, never mind the penicillin.

Eat, did we eat? How we ate! In China Town, we finally halted. Around one huge table, late at night, with the many coloured lanterns bobbing and ducking outside the window, feeling only just alive and no more, we each ordered a different dish and mixed and matched our spoonfuls. It was a feast of exotic and gargantuan proportions, after which we felt that we had well and truly tasted New York. For me, the personal highlight of those few days was the boat ride to the Statue of Liberty. I will never forget the sight of the lower New York skyline, including the new World Trade Center, with its antenna taller than the

Empire State Building. Sailing on the Island ferry, moving towards the Statue, as she lifted that arm and beacon skywards to welcome and embrace earth's 'huddled masses', not realising that she had engendered a new huddled mass of her own, I longed to share with that grand lady of freedom the words of Jesus, 'If the son shall make you free, you shall be free indeed' (John 8.36).

FREEDOM SONG

In search of freedom
Men go breaking chains,
Go shaking worlds
Of family, finance, state,
And bursting forth
From tired genealogy
Go shelving yesterday,
Not knowing as they flee
How soon the welcome beckons them
Into a tired tomorrow.
Yet there he stands,
The maker of all liberty,
'Twixt heaven and earth set free
To bend his will upon a stake of wood
No conscript he, but volunteer,
To spill his blood with royal impunity
And root upon the earth for every man a tree
Where each can quench the dragon breath of
    fear
And stand no more alone upon the sea.
But arm outstretched to heaven's Lord
Lift high the promise, and the challenge to be
    free.

Having survived the rigours of New York with the group I was keen to attempt a solo trip to view Niagara Falls in Canada. The Greyhound bus was certainly the fastest and most economical means of transport. The whole trip was completed in 24 hours, with the bus itself as my overnight accommodation on the return journey. The Falls were very different from how I had imagined them, but, nevertheless, not a disappointment. I had visualised all that pounding power of water cascading to its floor in the midst of fields and hills of scenic splendour. To discover that it was hedged in and about by twentieth-century commerce and urban suburbia came as quite a shock. However, I recognised that it was beautiful, not merely because of what it was, but because it was what it was, where it was.

My time in America was drawing to a close, and the final few days were a whirl of packing and visiting to say grateful goodbyes to my three sets of hosts and the many other friends I had made during my stay. On departure day the long journey home allowed time for another visit to Times Square and a less hurried wander along Broadway to 'give my regards', as dreamers do.

As I touched my hat to the neon signs for the last time, I mused that America had been an experience not to be missed. But I do not think God forged me in a shape that would advocate my taking up permanent residence.

There were interesting differences to remember. The sense of humour for one. For another, the way potatoes and steak and running gravy would be expected to share the same plate as equally runny ice-cream and jelly. Rain was to be stood out in to get cool and not run indoors away from. The different catch-phrases that were applicable: not 'Come in out of the rain', but 'Come in out of the bugs'. Mosquitoes, heat rash and spiders that bit like wolves and left hills on your leg big enough to climb. Indian chiefs in three-piece suits and lady ministers scuba-diving with snorkels. Being roused from bed at 1 a.m. to go shopping, in your pyjamas, in the car, at a drive-in store where it looked as though they might serve anything from a needle to an elephant, through the open car window, according to the McDonald's method. Oh yes, and then there was McDonalds and more McDonalds and more McDonalds and more Mc . . .

Breakfasting in the Big Apple on waffles and blueberries with syrup and cream. And corn fresh on the cob, dripping hot with butter and salt. And chocolate brownies, also hot, and as finger lickin' as any savoury.

Drive-in movies too, and churches, and motels, and just about anything else a car could reasonably get into without climbing stairs. And then there was the language barrier.

I recalled coming home after a hot and exhausting day's teaching. My third thoughtful hostess Sue offered to carry a chair outside to let me rest awhile before the evening meal. 'Where would you like to sit?' she asked. Now this was a lovely garden and quite large by my standards. It included flower beds, lawns and a vegetable garden, not to mention a veranda. I was spoilt for choice.

'I'd like to sit in the garden please,' I replied, waving my hand towards the rows of beautiful flowers. My hostess looked puzzled.

'The garden?' she queried.

'Yes,' I said in a voice rather smaller than before, wondering why she looked concerned. She shrugged and, with a degree of long-suffering, proceeded to carry my chair down the full length of the garden where she deposited it, incongruously, right in the middle of the cabbage patch. What patience the Americans have to indulge the ignorance of aliens! For I had not known at that stage that 'garden' here meant 'vegetable garden', and the flowers, trees and lawn belonged to the 'yard'.

We had a great laugh as I explained that 'yard', in Belfast, was a small space at the back of a house, enclosed on all sides by walls and usually accommodating the bin (sorry, trash-can), the washing, and the ancient redundant outdoor toilet. If it saw flowers at all, they would most probably be perched high in a window box. The yards of the Province were, in the main, definitely not the most salubrious of places to sit.

Throughout my stay, there had been many moments of hilarity and language differences, but what I learnt from America was how similar were the common experiences of the human race. The compassion and concern expressed for my homeland, the genuine hospitality and friendship extended to me, the joy and exhaustion of the Day Camp, the shared pain of trauma as I watched the drug addicts of Hope House grasp their last tenuous thread of life and struggle on living despite the odds.

Sadly, however, the first girl whom I met there died within a short time. She had been on heroin from her early teens and, when our leader asked if I could estimate her age, I guessed perhaps 45. She was 19. Hope is an old woman with wrinkled face and the heart of a child. In that house where I shared the love of Christ with sufferers who share, like us all, in the human condition of loneliness, they had the following meditation as their house philosophy.

HOPE PHILOSOPHY

We are here because there is no refuge finally
   from ourselves,
Until a person confronts himself in the eyes and
   hearts of others he is running.
Until he suffers them to share his secret he has
   no safety
Neither from himself nor from any other.
Afraid to be known
He will be alone.
Where else but in our common ground
Can we find such a mirror?
Here together a person can at last appear clearly
   to himself,
Not as the giant of his dreams,
Nor the dwarf of his fears,
But as a man part of a whole
With a share in its purpose.
In this ground we can each take root and grow,
Not alone anymore, as in death,
But alive to ourselves and to others.

Peace, The Philosophy of Hope House, Troy, New York State, USA.

3 ACROSS EUROPE

Belgium – Luxembourg – Germany – Bavaria
– Switzerland – Austria – Liechtenstein –
The Alps and Geneva – France

It was hard work acclimatising to the lonely but
hectic schedule of a Deaconess on call 24 hours a day.
Reading my 1976 diary again, after all this time, I am
amazed at the flurry of activity which I managed to
cram into those early years back in Northern Ireland.
I had returned from two years of training and community life-style in St Colm's College, Edinburgh to
be thrown headlong into the schedule of a large
urban parish. Life became a constant whirl of home
and hospital visits and worship services. Sermons had
to be prepared, and also lessons which I taught in
the schools. Valuable time was spent building rela-
tionships in the youth clubs and youth fellowship,
and all this successfully undertaken while struggling
to come to terms with living alone. Overriding the
timetable were the appointments for those in need of
counselling. Fulfilment was also mine, as individuals
were healed or made stronger by the grace of God,
and Carnmoney congregation did all in its power to
make me feel at home in friendship offered and
doors always open to my knock.

Nevertheless, by July I needed a holiday. I probably
needed a rest but, never having managed to learn
how to do that with finesse, I decided that I would
settle for a challenge instead.

Around Europe on my own in my second-hand Daf saloon in a month, sleeping as much as possible in the car to stretch the budget, seemed like a good idea at the time. Everyone who heard about my plans considered me quite mad – everyone, that is, except my father. True to form he sat down with me, as he had always done throughout my childhood when I suggested tree-climbing or any other potentially injurious activity. He would ask, 'Well, what can happen, Hilary?' When I had listed the broken arms and legs which might result from climbing that tree, he would, without smiling, mention in a low tone, 'Worse could happen, you could break your neck.' Then we would sit in silence for a while and that sombre thought would be allowed to sink in. Then he would say, 'Well, Hilary, are you prepared for the worst?' I would invariably nod. He would smile at me and say, 'Come on then, let's climb that tree.' The difference between then and now was that, in childhood, he would go with me and in his capable hands I knew the danger was greatly reduced.

This trip, however, would be undertaken alone. Dad and I had gone through the routine together. I had itemised all possible eventualities. That is, all the ones my youth and inexperience could envisage. The look in his eyes made me suspect that there were possibly several others I couldn't even imagine, but I didn't want to know. He scrutinised my face for a long time.

'Is it worth it, Hilary?' he asked.

'I've got to do this Daddy,' I said.

'Then do it,' he said. 'You will be full of regrets if you don't.'

The weeks leading up to my departure had been particularly demanding with a work schedule unusually pressurised for the month of July. Tuesday 29 June 1976 was the designated day of departure. I awoke that morning with car and case not packed and an emergency list of people to be visited in hospital. It was one of Ulster's rare good-weather days. Even in the summer it is normally a treat to enjoy very hot weather but today I knew the heat would only serve to make my preparations more difficult and exhausting. All day I rushed around in a pool of perspiration, trying to visit the various folk in hospital, in between getting my clothes aired and packed in fits and starts.

By 2 p.m. I was endeavouring to pack everything into the car. It took me two exhausting hours just to load the vehicle. I staggered up and down the flight of steps between my front door and the road with cases, food stores, cooking equipment, sleeping bag, my home-made curtain invention that stretched around the inside of the entire car, first-aid kit, engine repair kit, personal survival supplies for a whole month – to name but a few trifles. I expect an Antarctic expedition to the Pole might have travelled lighter.

Then, after another hectic round of the remaining hospitals, I finally managed to drive across town to my parents' home by 6 p.m., gulped down a hasty tea, loaded films in both my ordinary camera and cine (these were pre-video days), said my goodbyes and rushed to the boat.

Many a ship I have almost missed – but this embarkation was made even more dramatic. I raced across the empty loading car park realising that most of the passengers were already on board. Then, in my rear-view mirror, I caught a glimpse of a familiar car in pursuit. Screeching to a halt just short of the black awning of the ferry's hull, I turned my head to see my ashen-faced father dash from his car to mine waving a plastic bag. It contained my passport, maps, documents, money – in fact just about everything whose absence would have made the holiday impossible. I pictured the hall table I had left it on, near the door, just in case I would forget it. Shaking, I dashed onto the boat for Liverpool.

There was no seat left for me to sleep on all night. That old Liverpool ferry lacked many of the luxury features of its modern counterpart, and the long nine-hour sail through the night with engines pulsating in your ears was not to be anticipated with glee. Without a bunk it could be unpleasant enough, but without even a reclining seat in the lounge I dreaded the thought of attempting the marathon driving adventure ahead, having had a sleepless night to accentuate my already exhausted condition.

Although the boat was crowded, people didn't seem too rowdy so far. I wondered if their disposition would alter as the night progressed. Struggling to reception I made a desperate plea for a cabin. The rebuff was rude and discouraging but at least my name was added to the waiting list. Curled up on the drafty floor of the corridor for over an hour I had plenty of time to contemplate the perils ahead.

Right-hand driving, never before attempted. A second-hand car bought for a pittance, rattles and all. No overnight accommodation booked, as I had hoped to sleep mainly in the car. Strange people, strange countryside, strange customs, and the language? Another icy draught whistled round the edge of the boat deck and I shivered at the thought of the pathetic state of my school-girl French. What had seemed like exhilarating challenges were beginning to lose some of their allure. I recalled my father's pinched and anxious features as he sprinted across the car park with that plastic bag, and felt the full weight of the burden of worry which I had left with both my parents. They would be praying about now, I imagined. The thought both cheered me and filled me with guilt. Hadn't they enough to worry about, I thought, without my taking extra risks?

To take my mind off the thought I reached into my luggage and pulled out the map. I opened it and stared at its features and contours. It was a map of the world. Yes, I was about to drive across Europe using a map of the world. The laughter began somewhere in the pit of my stomach and slowly worked its way up my body till I was rolling back and forward in the aisle. The sheer ludicrous nature of the project struck me with force. Maybe the few other maps I had borrowed, of one or two of the countries en route, were in the car, or maybe they too had been left behind. Either way, at least I had a map of the world. I wiped the wet hilarity from my eyes and traced a damp finger from Ostend across to Austria and into Italy and made a sweeping circle home. I pictured myself driving off the ferry in France and asking the first person I saw, 'Excuse me, could you point me in the direction of Vienna?' It was then I prayed, through intermittent hiccups from laughing. I let God in on the joke and asked him to forgive me my foolishness and be with me on the journey. I didn't doubt that he would but, somehow, I had a feeling that this holiday was going to be no picnic. At that stage, I didn't know the half of it.

'McDowell!' the steward moved along the corridor shouting loudly. 'Berth for McDowell!' 'Here!' I replied, scrambling to my feet, and struggling over sleeping passengers, 'I'm McDowell, cabin for one?'

The steward looked at me disdainfully, 'You must be jokin' luv, it's a three-berth, and you're lucky to get this. A group of scouts couldn't make it and you got part of the cancellation.' Boy scouts doing me a good turn, I thought; so God was sharing the joke. I imagined him winking at me as I ploughed my way down the stairs into the bowels of the vessel to share the trip with a prospective foreign missionary, and another girl. I was grateful for the relative privacy of a cabin and my ship-mates were very pleasant, but the heat and stuffy conditions prevented me from sleeping a wink. I lay in a semi-conscious state until 3.30 a.m. and then needed a cool breath of air. Dressing quickly I made for the refrigeration of the deck where I half-sat, half-lay, shivering, until 5.30 a.m., watching the sea gradually divest itself of darkness and clothe itself in a crest of sunrise with just the merest hint of gull cry. It was glorious and I began to feel that, sleepy or not, this trip would be well worth the effort. God was there for me in the sunrise, and even in the fear and excitement of what lay ahead. I stood staring at the waves and gave myself fully to the adventure, knowing I would manage, but knowing I could do it only in God's strength.

Creator,
May I never look at water and see only liquid.
May I never stand by the ocean and fail to make communion with the sea.

Thank you for hope when there seems little reason to entertain it. For your strength when I am physically and mentally depleted.

Create in me a womb for your Spirit of adventure, and humour, and childlike wonder. Laugh with me, Lord, when all I can do is cry. *Amen.*

SEASCAPE

Dark liquid morning
Shine waves of noontide promise,
Caress me with dawn's touch.
Light's gentle creeping mastery
Eavesdropping on the waking day.
Washing me of fear and fantasy,
Rid me of mid-night dread,
Frozen spears of shadow
Bow in submission to the light.
Come heaven's orb entertain,
Be host to trust
And welcome in your timid guest of hope.

'Lord, you are the way,' I prayed as I sat in the driving seat of 'Daffe' watching the gaping hull of the Channel ferry yawn slowly wider to disgorge its cargo. 'Please God, be my navigator.' I wanted to go to Brugge (Bruges) and reckoned it was a very short hop from the boat but, for the first day I thought it was far enough to allow me to try my hand at driving on the 'wrong' side of the road, not to mention the challenge of finding a suitable b&b for my first night on the Continent.

Docks are confusing enough places at the best of times. I rolled off the ferry unslept and mapless. Every French sign was Greek to me and I wished I had paid more attention to my French teacher at school. The car in front was French too. 'Well,' I thought, 'he at least should know his way around.' The queue was moving slowly through the customs and I took the opportunity to send a telegram to the Boss.

At every roundabout, I hugged the back-bumper of

the car in front, and at every traffic light I performed as if he had me on tow. The poor man's nerves must have been in shreds by the time he and I both rounded a corner and I caught sight of the characteristic red roofs of the historical town of Brugge. He pulled over into a side-street and I passed him with my horn blaring and arms waving, yelling through my open window, 'Mercy, mercy beaucoup', at full lung-power. In the mirror I saw his puzzled expression and I daresay he dined out on stories of mad GB drivers with Irish registrations – but I like to think that the Lord will explain it to him someday when he is receiving his diadem in heaven.

I found a lovely bed and breakfast run by a community of sisters. On enquiring about a room for the night, I was told, 'Only one left, but it's up at the top of the house.' Each room had its own name and I asked, 'What is it called?' 'This one is St Patrick's room,' the sister replied. I knew I had come to the right place.

The stairs were hard to climb, but the view was spectacular. Laid out below me was a tapestry of crimson-coloured roofs carved in intricate patterns, a high proportion of which boasted bell and spire whose united, unpretentious discords erupted in peals of welcome at evensong and sunrise.

Before bed I felt so at home that I was able to settle to pen a letter to my family and reassure them of my safe arrival on foreign shores. The airmail, complete with stamps, was a present from one of the sisters who produced it when I asked for instructions on getting to the nearest post office to buy one. All my needs had been met by God, even down to the welcome mosquito net on the window. Before bed I was able to sit in that window gasping for the cool breeze, watching the sun set in resplendent illumination across the red roofs of Brugge, placed like rubies among the lush, green setting of the trees. The Lord had brought me to a safe place and I was fully at peace there.

SAFETY

Safety is knowing your companion,
Led Moses by cloud and fire, through desert
  pain.
Safety is knowing your pilgrim guide is a Saviour
Who will come again.
Learning to hear the whisper of Yahweh's mighty
  roar,
And battling through the waves to see the Son
  of God
Cook a meal of fish upon the shore.
Sleep safely when terror faced and conquered
Knows a Spirit, familiar and divine,
Yet despises not to rest with him,
In the anguished depths of humankind.

I am convinced that every road in Brussels must lead to the impressive Basilica. I found myself at its entrance several times and, finally, as it was midday, with the heat powerfully intimidating my progress, I abandoned, rather than parked, my car as close to the church's door as possible and stumbled into its saving coolness. The tide of dropped temperature washed over me like water to a dying man in the desert. It was wonderful.

The architecture was very beautiful, with exquisite stained-glass windows. It felt open, uncluttered and relatively modern. Little wickerwork chairs were reverently placed, but above all, I needed the coolness. The air was swept intermittently with the most beautiful, meditative music I had ever heard, and that too was iced refreshment.

There was no one around except God, and I knew he wouldn't mind, so I had my picnic, and then put four of the little chairs together adjoining a long, cold marble slab and stretched myself full-length for a most welcome sleep. Not surprisingly I was exhausted with the excitement, challenges and high temperatures of the past days and was so grateful for the inner and outer refreshment of the refrigerated silence of God's house.

Imagine my embarrassment to awaken, an hour later, surrounded by giggling children and adult visitors who were pointing to the sign on the wall above me and then to my prostrate form which now galvanised itself into action and attempted a translation of the legend which (I discovered) read, 'Give to poor children', and nearby the text, 'Come unto me all who labour and are heavy laden and I will give you rest' (Matt. 11.28). They must have thought I was a visual aid for the message. I certainly did not accept the coins they held out to me in eager little palms, but I like to think that the poor box in the Basilica was more full than usual that day, thanks to my visit.

Red-faced I hastily left, thanking God for his rest. He and I laughed about it together and the laughter was part of the refreshment that I needed. All day I remembered how true are his promises and how he fulfils them in the most practical of ways. I had desperately needed coolness and rest, I came to him, and there, in his house, he gave me exactly what I needed. Thank you Boss – you did it again.

A MILLION WAYS TO REST

They've never been here, Lord,
Those cheerful, giggling, faces,
Enjoying the humour of my rest.
Never been to the battle of the perspiration,
Soaking every cell and waging war on thought
As headaches fight for mastery of sanity,
And legs feel like manacled tombstones
Rooted in the graveyard of optimistic plans.
They don't know yet that Heaven can time-share
    with the earth,
Permitting even Hell to sow its conquered sample
In physical exhaustion at the planet's edge.
This edge they see in me,
Stretched full-length upon the marble slab.
Yet what they see is only humour
And a strangeness born of unknown pain.
Unknown to their shining, untouched faces,
They'd help me if they could.
But just for now I can assist them with a smile.
They ask no more. And when God said,
'Come and I shall give . . .'
I have an odd sensation
That he had more in mind than ease of bone.
'Be a child again, my daughter, entertain the little
    ones,
And share a joke with me.'

On the drive to Luxembourg – the city where pop
radio-music culture originated, on a station which
had often kept me company as I drove – I did battle
with the traffic and the maps and the heat, not to
mention a king-sized bee who invaded the car and
would not leave.

Arriving at the youth hostel at 1 p.m. I discovered that all was closed for shut-eye. The continuous, soaring temperature was claiming my last ounce of energy and I sat in a kind of heat-exhaustion stupor until tea-time.

By 8 a.m. the following day, after a reasonable night's sleep, I drove from the youth hostel in high spirits to begin a full day of sightseeing, believing I might move on to Germany the next day. Two miles later the car stopped. It just stopped. The petrol gauge was showing low and I thought that fuel was the problem, although it did not seem completely empty. However, all other gauges were normal and there seemed no other explanation. As I came to a halt a man was crossing the road just in front of me. He seemed an angel sent from God because, not only did he go to the nearest garage to fill his cans with petrol and bring them back for me, but, when it still refused to go, he went and phoned the AA.

On the arrival of the AA man the engine was opened for the first time since leaving Britain, and he shook his head in the way mechanics do when they are ready either to announce a phenomenal bill, or pronounce the death sentence on the unsuspecting vehicle. He made clicking noises between tongue and teeth, and spread his hands wide in desperation. Despite my language problems there was no misunderstanding the universal language of mime. 'Kaput!' he said with emphasis. Now that I did understand, for kaput is kaput in any language. I hoped fervently that he was exaggerating. 'Not kaput,' I said. 'Non kaput,' I repeated, disgracefully experimenting in cross-language semantics. He rolled his eyes and stamped the ground, 'Kaput, *kaput*,' he shouted. I was beginning to get the message.

The oil-cap was missing from the engine and everything was thickly covered in oil. I had no lubricant left and the engine had seized. I'm no car mechanic, but even I knew that this meant well and truly kaput.

'But why did the oil-warning light not show?' I asked the poor mechanic who was struggling to communicate with me in broken English. He stared at me in bewilderment. 'Look,' I said, trailing him by the elbow to the dashboard. 'No light, no warning.' He examined the wiring and found it to be faulty, while I stood silently begging the Boss, 'What do I do now, Lord?'

The man ushered me into his AA van and we went for oil. I found myself actually quite enjoying the drive as I could view the city without wrestling with the traffic. But back at the car it still wouldn't start. Off went my rescuer assuring me that the local Daf garage-man would come with a truck to take me to the garage in about an hour. There was obviously nothing else I could do, so I took refuge in the doorway of an old church. The building itself was locked but the shady graveyard provided coolness and peace. How grateful I was to God that this was beside my breakdown point, at the time of the midday heat. I comforted myself with a meagre picnic of crisps and Fanta, and prayed for help for what lay ahead.

One hour later, almost to the minute, the breakdown truck came and I enjoyed another effortless drive through this beautiful city. On arrival at the garage the full implication of what had happened awaited me – and it was quite a shock. I would have to buy a new engine! The cost would be 18,000 francs (about £240 at that time) and that is not the kind of currency I was accustomed to carrying around in my pocket, even on a Continental holiday. For a

Deaconess at that time it was a sizeable amount of money. I counted my travellers cheques and cash but they amounted to less than the equivalent of 9,000 francs. What was I to do? Without the car, I was well and truly grounded. They appeared to be polite enough people, but were obviously not prepared to wait all day for my decision.

The garage staff said they would try and find me a second-hand engine which would cost less, about 14,000 francs, so I would only need to ask my bank to send around 7,000 francs. 'Only,' I thought, with the trip a mere few days old and the lion's share of the journey still to come.

A lady drove me to the bank, which directed us to the post office, which then shunted us on to the GPO. Finally, I succeeded in sending a telegram to my bank at home, hoping that the money could be sent directly to the garage. Thankfully I was provided with a taxi back to the youth hostel, tired, hot and without visible means of support. I booked in for a third night, and longed for a speedy repair.

In peak season three nights were the maximum allowed at each youth hostel. They seemed quickly used up. There I stood at the door, surrounded by my luggage and still no car. A Good Samaritan found a taxi for me. So, with the last of my paper money I paid my way to the garage. I sat on a low bench; a few feet in front of me was a narrow counter where people came and went to pick up spare parts or make car maintenance appointments, and to my right, a few feet away, was a huge cardboard cut-out of an Eskimo boy callously holding out an ice-cream to unsuspecting tourists like me, stranded, penniless, in soaring temperatures. I apologise to those who have known what real torture is like, but I have to say that, as I sat dehydrating slowly for the full day, with this pesky wee Eskimo grinning at me as he extended that ice-cream in my direction, I had to concentrate pretty hard on my praying to stay cool, and pray I did.

By lunch-time the money still hadn't come and I discovered that the repair to my motor had not even started: they were waiting for the money to arrive first. The Bad 'un tempted my mind to panic and I knew I must distract myself somehow in order not to slide into despondency. Eat, I thought, that's it, I'll make an effort to cook lunch. I had not been allowed use of the car to sleep in – apparently there was some fear that I might drive it away in the night, without an engine – but I was permitted to take out the cooking paraphernalia and boil my kettle. Attaining access to my little store of eggs and tinned luncheon meat was like discovering the Hanging Gardens of Babylon. In the midst of the dirty, unhygienic diesel-oil surroundings of a garage workshop floor, I spread my tea-towel of rough cotton and luxuriated in the aroma of a freshly boiled egg and full tin of luncheon meat. It was wonderful, and it could have been the Ritz. I thanked God for that moment and tried not to think about the night ahead. It was just as well that I enjoyed this meal, as it was to be my only food until breakfast the next day. By nightfall the money had still not arrived.

The garage was closing now: the innocuous sounds of locking-up procedures and the casual, normal good-night exchanges, sounded particularly ominous in my present predicament. I might well have ended up sleeping under a hedge if God had not led me to the British Embassy. There I met Maddy, a member of staff, who treated me to a warmth of welcome and kindness for which I will be forever grateful. Free phone-calls to Belfast, to expedite the money, and a proper hotel for the night.

After the luxury of a full eight hours of uninterrupted sleep, I was treated to a wonderful breakfast the next day with a full pot of tea which tasted to me, in my dehydrated state, like nectar from heaven itself, and then a free taxi back to the Embassy. All afternoon I waited, in comfort this time. The day's papers had arrived from London and I read voraciously, hungry for news of Northern Ireland. By closing time I was still at the Embassy, but the money was not. Four days now I had been stranded, waiting. It had been a real exercise in patience. Perhaps the Lord knew that I needed the practice.

Not being able to afford to extend my stay at the hotel and, as I was loath to be a burden to the Embassy indefinitely, I asked Maddy if there was anywhere inexpensive where I could stay tonight. Her voice was slightly hesitant when she said, 'There's the convent.' It sounded more like a question than a suggestion. I was quick on the uptake, believing that her reticence had something to do with her knowledge of Northern Ireland, perhaps based upon media reports of our assumed prejudice and bigotry. 'Great,' I grinned. 'That sounds good. I can share with them all about my work as a Deaconess. I'm sure the sisters would be interested.'

Having found the front door, I had to wait awhile at what I took to be the main entrance, and stood there practising a little speech in my best school-girl French. 'I am alone, I am in trouble. Please may I stay the night?' Even though it was not possible to converse at length because of the language barrier, I received a warm welcome and was given a modern, airy room and sat down to a delicious meal. The surroundings felt more like a hospital than a convent. In addition to the sisters there was a group of other women dining, a high proportion of whom were obviously looking forward to an imminent happy event, and I felt sorry for them having to carry the extra weight in the midst of such excessive summer heat.

I attempted to develop a conversation by producing my Deaconess badge and, still in school-girl French, started to explain that I was employed, in a fully commissioned work of the Lord in the Church. To my horror, expressions changed from puzzlement to distress. One ran from the room, her hands covering her face, mumbling something about the situation being much worse than she had thought. I was devastated. Could Luxembourg be as bad as Belfast, I wondered? Had I made an awful mistake in coming here? I only wanted to share the joy of the Lord with others and especially those dedicated to obeying God within the service of the diaconate. I came to the conclusion that the fault lay with my inadequate grasp of the language. By nightfall, at last, I had found someone who spoke English. I explained about the vision for my trip across Europe, about the disastrous breakdown with the car, the four, now to be five days, stranded in Luxembourg, and my desire to share about my faith and work with the sisters.

The listener's eyes grew wider, her mouth relaxed into a broad smile and finally, before I had finished, she was laughing. I did not really see what was so funny, but it was infectious and I laughed too, it was such a relief to be communicating again.

'What door did you come in?' she asked. It seemed a strange question.

'Pardon?'

'When you arrived at the convent, which door?' she repeated.

'The front one,' I said. She smiled warmly.

'Have you ever seen the one at the back?' I had not.

'Then take a look at it before you leave,' she said. 'It is the main entrance for the patients.'

On my way to the other door I kept thinking, 'Patients, she said, patients.' Slowly, it was beginning to dawn on me. Sure enough, at the back door there was the information telling me that this was a hostel for homeless women, many of whom were single mothers and single mothers-to-be. I suppose if a person arrives at a hostel for unmarried mums announcing, 'I am alone, I am in trouble, can I stay here?' – well what did I expect? I imagined St Peter and all the angels banqueting out on that one for a long time to come. I enjoyed much warmth and hospitality in that place.

KINGDOM TONGUE

What language do I need
To speak the Kingdom tongue?
Does it bear the nuance of St Patrick,
The complexities of Paul?
Shall harmony of Francis make it sing?
Will the wrestling of an Augustine,
The doctrine of John Knox,
Make it clear to my companions
I'm a daughter of the King?

When all the tongues are tied, Lord,
When human speech is dumb,
Will spirit burst from tomb of bondage?
Breaking manacles of mind?
Shall love be given utterance to sing?
Will the struggle of a loneliness,
The pain of humankind,
Make a sacrifice of kindness,
Amongst children of the King?

Back at the Embassy in the morning, I received the
wonderful news that the money had arrived. In fact,
as they had forgotten to cancel the original telegram,
I was now the proud owner of twice the necessary
amount. God really does have a sense of humour. As
I stood in the garage, staring at my new, reconditioned
engine with my pockets full of traveller's cheques, I
weighed up the possible choices. Turn back now and
go straight home, before anything worse happens? Or
go on and finish the adventure in God's strength,
trusting him to be with me for the remainder of the
journey, as he had been throughout the disaster?

I found a quiet, smelly, greasy, oil-stained place to
pray. Remembering the difficulties of heat and
exhaustion and car breakdown, and recalling also
the joys of friendships along the way, I decided that,
on my journey, I was not among strangers but friends
to whom God had chosen to introduce me. I wanted
to meet them all. I wanted to go where he was leading.
'No man,' said Jesus, 'who puts his hand to the
plough and looks back, is fit for the Kingdom of
God' (Luke 9.62). I knew that, when the Lord spoke
those words, he was referring to the spiritual journey

of faith and servanthood, and it did not necessarily mean that we should not turn away from a course which proves wrong, but this journey, to me, had been sanctified by the Lord's endorsement and provision thus far. He had arranged for the car to be fixed and money to be provided. How could I throw in the towel now? I knew I must go on.

By lunch-time I bade my farewells to the garage staff. They wished me good luck, and I wished for God speed instead, and climbed into the driving seat. I felt somewhat shaky turning the vehicle into the Continental traffic once again. After a number of days off the road it was rather frightening to feel again as I did during my first hours on the 'wrong' side of the road. However, the blue Daf saloon, Daffe to his friends, zoomed along with seemingly effortless composure, much quieter and smoother than usual. All afternoon I drove, crossing yet another border without even noticing. Suddenly, I was in Germany and the scenery had changed. I had freed myself from the motorways for a while and relinquished the fertile, gentle hills of farming land in Luxembourg, with its gorgeous small forests strewn with azure carpets, thanks to a little flower akin to a bluebell. Now, from Trier, I was on the Rhine, and it was beautiful.

Much green, stalk-like vegetation surrounded me and I wondered if I was seeing my first vines. I tried to film a lady working among them and she came at me with a farming implement of hostile proportions. I left swiftly, wishing again that I could speak the lingo. The hills grew higher, but not enormous, and their expanse was sweeping. The valleys nurtured delightful little canals of the Rhine at every turn with big tug-like boats continually shuffling their length. It took a great deal of driving to reach Darmstadt.

I had been told wonderful stories of the Lutheran Sisters of Darmstadt, a nursing order of Deaconesses, and I was eager to meet them and learn of their work. That night they gave me my very own apartment overlooking Frankenstein's Castle. The welcome was from a neat, calm lady in grey with a little white cap who delivered a hot supper with the warmth of friendship shared by those who minister within the world-wide diaconate. I learned about the sisters' work in the clinic for elderly folk before enjoying my luxurious bathroom and a good night's sleep.

The next day I drove the short distance to Würzburg. This was the city which afforded me the chance to attempt my first camping experiment in the car.

The site was beside a river and, although the walking back and forward to the distant washrooms required much effort and was not without difficulties, yet the experiment, I felt, would be a success. The actual sleeping in the car was really quite comfortable.

Once I had fought off the mosquitoes; and struggled with the Kosangas calor-gas stove to make my evening meal; and scalded myself from the camping cooker; and played hide-and-seek with the curtain rail that kept falling down, mid-coiffure; and squiggled and wriggled into my pyjamas with one hand, holding the torch with the other, carefully positioning it not to throw a shadow of myself on to the thin curtains – yes, sleeping was actually reasonably comfortable. Comfortable, that is, until the five fellows in the adjoining camper decided this was too much fun to miss. They must have observed the blue Daf bobbing up and down enthusiastically at my every turn and twist, because I was just drifting off to sleep when Daffe began to do his own acrobatics. Up and down went the back axle and then the singing started. Were the boys drunk, I wondered, or just high-spirited? One moved to the front and lay across the bonnet trying to find a chink in my curtains with his torch. I was very thankful that I could not understand the language, because I would rather not know the meaning of the taunts and jibes which punctuated their cat-calls. I lay very still and was grateful for locked doors and windows closed tight to exclude mosquitoes and other pests.

I prayed that they would get bored and move away. They bounced the car up and down and I prayed the brakes would hold. They hammered on the windows and I prayed the curtains wouldn't fall. One of them crawled underneath and treated the undercarriage to an impersonation of bongo drums. Daffe, having recently suffered engine failure, came close to heart failure – not to mention his driver. 'It's just high spirits,' I whispered to the Lord. 'Please let it be just high spirits.' I thought of that river, so picturesque, a few yards away. I had parked as close as I could to it for the scenery and the cool sound of water. Their voices were now drowning out even that. I speculated how difficult it would be to remove a Daf saloon from a river. With a fleeting thought I tried to estimate the depth of the water. It had not looked too deep, but then . . .

Bang, one of them had fallen off the car, attempting to climb onto the roof. Maybe they were drunk after all. I did not want to end up in the river, in the car. But then, would it be wise to get out of the car? I decided against it. Sit tight, I thought, and let God handle this.

A radio crackled into song. It was rock music and much too loud. Another of the boys yanked on the door handle at my ear, as I lay prone and silent. He was shouting something in time to the music. If he wants a dance, I thought, he is out of luck on more counts than one. The humour of it made me smile, and I thanked God for that. I heard a door open and slam shut on the far side of the car. I remembered the lovely family of four who had parked their caravan on that side. The father was shouting loudly in the boys' language. Heated retorts on both sides ensued, and torches blazed around the car. The boys stopped rocking Daffe and the father called to me through the driver's window in broken English.

'Everything OK, Miss?'

'Yes,' I replied as strongly and as confidently as I could.

'I am just going to sleep now', I said. 'Thank you.'

'Goodnight,' he said.

'Goodnight,' I replied.

'Goodnight,' retorted five cheery voices, in unison as they retreated to their camper, singing as they went. I slept, they slept, thank the Lord, we all slept peacefully in our own places. Safe, for the night.

LULLABY

Rock-a-bye Baby
On the tree top,
If the bough breaks
The cradle will fall,
And down will come baby
And cradle and all.

Rock-a-bye Hilary
At water's edge,
If the brakes fail
The cradle will fall,
And wet will be Hilary
And cradle and all.

Rock-a-bye Baby
Father's a God,
He made the bough
Where all cradles rest,
So trust to sleep Baby
Try faith at the test.

In the morning, it was with renewed confidence, despite my adventure, that I cooked breakfast in the open air and set off for Munich, sightseeing at the famous clock tower with its delicately crafted figures who dance as the hour strikes. Salzburg followed and on to Vienna, which I realised would be the midway stage and turning-point of my travels. Due to the unforeseen delay in Luxembourg I faced the inevitable decision that there would be no Italy on this trip.

Although it was a long way, the driving was very easy indeed. Downhill most of the way, with the wind behind me, Daffe fairly zoomed along. The time-consuming part was, as usual, the attempt to find a hostel. In Vienna, I found one in a lovely old building decorated with frescos. It had real character, was set in beautiful grounds and, as I had reached the turning-point in the journey, I decided to stay three nights.

Vienna offered a great deal in the way of music and culture and beauty. I was determined to enjoy the next two days to the full, and enjoy them I did.

That is, once I had worked out how to survive the frustrating one-way system. The city is huge, and seemed to be made up of a million plazas, leading to more plazas, leading to more plazas. A veritable warren of irregular zigzagging confusion. It took two hours to make a journey that should have taken 20 minutes. Nevertheless, Vienna presented to me her trophies. It was a kind of chance happening of sights. Except I do not believe in either chance or coincidence, and I believe I have the Lord to thank for each new treasure he let me experience.

Museums, palaces, art galleries, gardens and most of all, many, many, fountains. The place was awash with them. But would I ever find the famous Schönbrunn Palace, the summer residence of the ancient Austrian royalty? After a chat with the Boss, I decided just to follow the flow of traffic and see where it took me. It led to the longest and best shopping street in Vienna, the Mariahilferstrasse, where I found a snack café for lunch, which served me a glass of cold milk, yes, real milk to drink. Until now no one would believe that I actually wanted to drink milk. They would inevitably say,

'Milk – goat's milk?'

'No,' I would reply.

'Buttermilk?' they would venture.

'No,' I would sigh, 'cow's milk.'

And then I would launch into a humorous mime sequence of milking procedures, punctuated by the odd 'Moo', which had never failed to get me an appreciative audience but, until now, no milk.

I stood there gulping down the wonderfully refrigerated white nectar until a small child, about three years old, who had been staring at me in incredulous, wide-eyed wonder, suddenly burst into floods of

58

tears. 'What did I do?' I asked the mother. She smiled sympathetically and pointed to my now empty glass, replying, 'He has not seen an adult drinking milk before.' Well, welcome to an alien culture, Hilary! I tried not to drink milk again in the presence of toddlers. St Paul did warn us not to offend the weaker brethren, but I never thought it would lead to this!

My quest for the Palace ended so simply this time. I discovered that this long and impressive shopping street led directly to the Schönbrunn. Despite the excessive heat I walked quite a distance through the grounds, and then took the official guided tour of the inside. I really enjoyed seeing the grandeur. Even the stoves were decorated with gold. Walking through rooms of porcelain and jade, Japanese and Chinese, I wondered about the people who had moved through these rooms, the nobility who had taken all this for granted, who had spilt their tea out of cups that were now priceless antiques, spilt it onto silken cushions, wiped it from floor-coverings imported from Japan. I imagined the conversations which had echoed around these walls. How much childish glee had resounded along these corridors? Had laughter or tears been the sound most often heard? All I saw were inanimate objects, the cold trappings of lives long gone. Their artefacts influenced me less than their personalities might have done, if I had been granted either the fortune or misfortune to have known them during the time when they were each given one brief chance to touch the earth, on the way through.

Did they ever look up, I wondered? Look up beyond the dumb gold, the inarticulate porcelain, the expensive drapes hanging motionless now? Where did they touch the life beyond? I raised my eyes from the Palace door to view the long, symmetrical baroque gardens. They were interesting, in an organised, computer-programmed sort of way, and there ahead lay the impressive arched splendour of the Gloriette, a large, pillared monument on the top of the hill.

It seemed to beckon me. Surely the inhabitants would have climbed up there to gain spiritual vision. Its drawing-power was almost magnetic. Could I make it to the top? I had already walked a long way that day, both around the gardens and through the house. The heat was stifling and I wondered if I could do it.

The guide book stated that a series of paths lead up 'gentle grassy slopes to the hill crowned by the Gloriette'. Unfortunately I took the guide book at its word, to my cost. The word 'gentle' did not apply. Probably, to an ordinary person, they were graceful and gently sloping – but not to me! The first part of the walk was along the lovely flower garden; that could reasonably be described as a walk, but still not easy for me in the excessive heat. A beautiful fountain stood at the end of this section of the path, and I rested, staring up at the second half of the journey. This next section was no walk. It was, for me, quite definitely a climb. However, as always, I considered that there should be no turning back. The steep slope ahead now bore all the hallmarks of a challenge.

Two paths separated to circle in opposite directions around the hill. I chose the shorter, if steeper climb, believing it would be better to return by the long, winding and presumably more gradual, descent.

The path I chose went straight up like a ladder, but at least it was well sheltered by trees and afforded a welcome coolness for the struggle. I strained forward, grasping at tree-trunks, branches, anything to steady my balance and advance my progress. I dared not stop – merely to attempt to turn around would have been to lose my balance and go hurtling down the slope again.

EVEREST II

Thanks for the climb, Lord,
It could have been smoother,
The rocks didn't need to savage my toes,
My hands now in ribbons from knife-edged tree
    branches,
My hair streaked in straggles clings to my neck.
And where did this elephant come from,
The one hitching a lift on the rise of my chest?
Wind-tossed and wheezing and frightened of
    hurtling
Backwards on gravel, cheek bottom,
Dry-ski to the ground.
Did I have to compete with Sir Edmund?
'What's in a name?' they said at my birth!
Is this the pain that conquered Everest?
Dripping with sauna awash on my back?

Thanks for the climb, Lord,
No prize at the top.
What crazy compulsion pushed me to the
    summit?
Whose idea was this anyway?
Whose idea, Lord, say now?
It was yours, said the Lord,
Your idea my child,
And you got to the top,
Because I came for the ride.

Finally I reached the top and turned to look downwards for the first time. But what a disappointment! I discovered that the view was not as spectacular as I had imagined it might be. I had to remind myself that it's not the view that makes it worthwhile, but the climb itself. It was reward enough to have met the challenge.

The next evening I attended an open-air concert at the *Rathaus* (town hall). I arrived early, yet the square was already half-filled. It was lovely to see folk of every colour and nationality strolling languidly in and out through the pillars of the courtyard, admiring the flags of all nations and greeting friends. I felt relaxed and on holiday at last. I lay back in my seat, closing my eyes and, as darkness fell, let the coolness of the night and the genius of Beethoven wash me clean from the stress of my journey so far. It felt as though my refreshment was almost complete. All I need now, Lord, I prayed, is a friend with whom to share this lovely evening. I was only wishing, really. Ireland was a long way away and I did not seriously expect my wish to be granted. But the Lord knows when wishes are needs, and all needs are prayers to him. What a wonderful God we have; his surprises are the best ones ever.

Only two rows in front, his provision was already there and I didn't even know it. She spotted me first, and came to my side, rousing me with a hug. It was Lucy, an American youth-hosteller who had been a friend to me in Luxembourg. What a delight the reunion was – so unexpected, so seemingly accidental – just when I was feeling the pain that only beauty brings, and needing to share it with a friend.

After the concert Lucy and her girlfriend and I had supper together, and then I headed back to the hostel, in the dark this time, which brought its own misgivings. But God had crafted me a great day and he allowed nothing to spoil it. I found home-base quite easily in comparison with previous attempts. Thank you Lord, for Vienna. Tomorrow it would be time to turn my car in the direction of home. The half-way point had been safely reached and celebrated in proper style.

THE PAIN THAT ONLY BEAUTY BRINGS

Muse of high degree
Come dance, come play with me,
Come rest within the crevice of my soul,
Let me taste the joy of your designs,
Ingest the wonder of your grace
Till hunger has no place within my being.
How did you touch Beethoven's heart?
And deaf ears flood with sound?
Crafting the pain that only beauty brings
To scatter heaven's seed upon earth's stony
    ground.

How did you spill the water onto earth
To baptise old to second birth?
And burst the chrysalis to let the insect fly?
And in its flight let wind-tipped prisms of the
    light
Sprinkle tears to eyes long dry from weeping,
Till they fear no more to let the hurting in
And raising shaded lids risk injury once more,
Embracing pain that only beauty brings,
And in the healing of the scars, their God adore?

4 HOMEWARD BOUND

Liechtenstein – Switzerland –
The Black Forest – France – Luxembourg

Liechtenstein afforded me another night's camping –
and another mini-breakdown when my exhaust fell
off. Again God provided Good Samaritans to help
me on my way. The following morning was misty
and I was rained out of the royal Principality. The
search was on for high, snow-capped pinnacles. I
wanted to drink the iced air with gasps of inner-city
thirst, and be deafened by the silence of endless
space above me, reaching towards the heavens, where
I could imagine eagles flying unseen.

After Zurich the road twisted upwards through
the mountains, but, ironically, I could not see one,
not one. The clinging, wet mist masked everything
beyond the confines of the car. If it hadn't been for
the steep gradient, steadily rising, beneath Daffe's
wheels, I could have believed I was driving through
a flat, uninteresting valley. But the road kept climbing and twisting and winding itself around those
shrouded giants. Passing through Lucerne, where I
had spent a holiday with my parents some years previously, I scanned the horizon for Mount Pilatus, but
not even a pale shadow was visible. Only my memory
assured me of its presence, but the lake and picturesque bridge brought back a surge of reminiscence
that was almost a physical pain. Was it home-sickness,

I wondered, or the absence of my parents this time?

By mid-afternoon I had reached Interlaken and booked in at another lovely camp-site. Remembering the joy of my first visit to the mountain called Grindelwald First, I headed in that direction and saw, at last, the snow-capped peaks for which I longed. The sun came out long enough to let me stand in the snow and remember. Remember how Mum and Dad and I had ridden the two-seater chair-lift to the top of the mountain. Dad and I in one chair, with me hanging over the side to get a spectacular shot with my cine camera, and Mum in the other, some distance away, signalling wildly with both arms. I waved back, not realising that the strap of my camera was flapping far beneath me, brushing the tops of the Christmas trees below us. In ignorance, I kept waving to her enthusiastically and brought some great shots home in my camera. I dread to think what would have happened if a branch had hooked into that camera strap. I don't think I could have let go, and there was only one narrow bar across the front of the chair to stop the passengers from tumbling to the ground.

I remember the thrill of discovering how warm it was at the top of the mountain. Hot sunshine and yet snow-drifts by the path which were taller than I was. It was a wonderland to me, and even more so when my father took a stick and wrote my name in large letters in the snow. 'There,' he said, 'there's more than one Hilary who can climb mountains.' I knew what he meant and I will be forever grateful to him for his continual encouragement. Today I took a stick and wrote 'Thank you, Dad' in large letters in the snow.

Tonight I faced another evening of camping and

was glad to have no difficulty bedding down in the car this time.

All night it rained, and I mean *rained*, with a capital R. The thought of trying to unstick Daffe and myself from mud in the morning was none too appealing. Fortunately, when I peeped from my idiosyncratic curtaining arrangement, the dawn was both dry and promising. By 7.30 a.m. I was speeding towards Geneva in search of the famous water-spurt of Lake Geneva.

I am sure there must be several routes between Interlaken and Montreux; however, the way that I chose to go was not effortless. It was both glorious and treacherous. I had seen mountains before, but these ones were huge. The mist had lifted and the surroundings blasted me with their magnificence. However, I had to drive across this range of iced sabres in a Daffe whose reputation so far was none too reassuring. It was nerve-wracking negotiating each twist of the passes' serrated edges and bottomless drops.

But I had as yet underestimated what God had in store for me. I thought I was just getting from A to B on the journey. But the Father wanted to show me beauty, real beauty.

Have you ever been alone, submerged in a cupped valley of alpine wonder, far above sea level, far distant from the sound of a human voice? Where the silence is overpowering, and the beauty is almost too much for the human soul to bear? When you cry out to the Lord in your smallness and your wonder, 'God this is awesome, there can be no greater glory than this', and from the depth of the far-distant ravine comes a low rumble, and then a gradual change creeps over the sky, and the Lord sends a thunderstorm?

I had seen Continental thunderstorms before, one in Luxembourg, and one in Vienna, but this one, this one the Lord himself was enjoying. For half-an-hour I took the gift of it, full blast, in the mountains, his unfettered lantern-show of light and steam. He made me breathless with it, as the echo-chamber of the mountains bounced his glory to my very soul. Dramatic purple and blue illumination against the purity of whiteness, rumbling endlessly through the hills as if to roll his message as far as the earth's end and back. Echoes of a thousand voices, and yet all one and all one still. The way he lit those trees made a mockery of the sun, and I knew that day that I had never seen a tree before.

HIS GLORY MIRRORED

'No greater glory?'
No greater Glory, child!
Your eyes cannot see, nor perceive
The splendour I hold hostage
Awaiting my command.
Can you imbibe even the mildest drop of my
    elixir?
Discern the smallest sonance of the echo of my
    voice?
I withold my majesty in deference to your
    human frailty,
Can you endure unfettered pain that beauty
    brings?
This millet-seed of beauty, earth-type wonder,
Will mustard seed of faith your wonder grow,
But only with the eyes of mine inheritance
Can you reach forth, entrust your love,
And in Christ's full embrace my glory know.

It was lunch-time when I arrived in Geneva. A Belfast friend had given me the address of a friend of hers in the city, and by mid-afternoon I had found the apartment, uncertain of the reception I would receive, as my visit was unheralded. I was desperate for a chat with a native from Northern Ireland again, and gladly waited for the rest of the afternoon outside her flat.

Nevertheless I began to worry about what I would do if she didn't return home. Perhaps she was away on holiday? It's one thing to spend the night in the car in a recognised camp-site; it is quite another to curl up by the side of a city street. In the midst of my anxiety I saw again the glory of that morning's thunderstorm, the faces of those helpers, numbering quite a few by now, who had aided my path and helped me on my way thus far from Belfast to Geneva. I recalled again the touch of my Lord in the mountains and knew that my Saviour was as real here, by the kerbside of a city pavement, as elsewhere. 'Show me the innocent joys of this city too, Lord,' I prayed, 'and bring the lady home by tea-time, please.'

At 6 p.m. on the dot the lady came home to find a tired, but shining-eyed and thankful, guest upon her doorstep. Isobelle, to her great credit, did not throw me out.

After tea my thoughts turned to camp-sites but my hostess invited me to stay and so out came my sleeping bag. The settee proved to be a good deal more comfortable than either the car or the youth hostels had been. It was wonderful to be in a real home again, and with a fellow Northern Ireland citizen. Just to speak without carefully slowing my sentences or picking the most widely understood word was a real delight. I could use Ulster phrases like, 'How's about ya!' and instead of 'Hello' say, 'Is this where you are?', and when told something of amazement respond with an incredulous 'Get away!' without having to use subtitles. Even my hands got a temporary rest from miming. Though, come to think of it, they rarely rest, regardless.

It was a great relief knowing where I would sleep that night, a luxury indeed. But the evening still had gifts for me to enjoy and God had not forgotten my prayer. 'Come on,' said my hostess after tea. 'Wouldn't you like to see Geneva by night?' Wouldn't I just!

As a passenger now, with Isobelle's wheels below us, relaxed without having to heed the road signs, or the one-way streets, or the map, I was driven through a veritable wonderland of illumination. Ringed full around the lake, the lights twinkled and glistened and the little trees stood resplendent in the floodlit dazzle of their own reflection in the water. Holiday-makers and locals strolled together along the narrow streets of the quaint old part of the city. The older the building, the more it snuggled close to its neighbour in a vain attempt to escape the dazzle of the brightly-lit boats in the growing dusk. As twilight turned to darkness, there was no escaping the incredible artificial shining of Geneva's chic designer stores along the boulevards. 'Thank you Father,' I prayed. 'It's all lovely, but after this morning, I know the difference between this light and the light which produces the pain that only beauty brings.'

Where is the 'spurt' I wondered? I had come to see the famous *Jet d'Eau*, the wonderful fountain which I had often seen on TV, spurting high into the air from the lake. Hadn't I heard it was the highest one in Europe – or was it the world? 'It's off,' I was told. 'You've missed it,' said a local citizen shaking his head sadly and looking as if he would personally have switched it on for me if that had been within his power. I smiled and assured him, 'It's alright, I will see it tomorrow before I leave the city. I want to catch it at the very moment it is switched on.' I did not want to miss that incredible surge which sends it sky-high as the switch is thrown. The man shook his head slowly: 'You will have to be up early,' he said. 'I have lived here all my life and have never caught the very moment when it spurts. You must watch and watch and never take your eyes off the lake for a moment, or you will miss something special.'

The next morning, early, I sat alone by the side of the water, having said goodbye to my Belfast hostess, pinning my eyes resolutely on the spot across the lake where I had been told to look. I stared and stared for a very long time, scared to glance away or scratch my nose. My eyes began to cross, then a squint developed as my sight blurred with the concentration. I conjectured, 'What if I was staring at the wrong spot?' I knew that the direction was right, but supposing I had misunderstood all those waving arms and garbled instructions? What if this was Bank Holiday for water-spurts? What if the man who turns it on was sick? Or the council had declared a water shortage and imposed a hosepipe ban? Or what, I mused, if my two eyes go completely cross-eyed just at the very moment when the . . . Suddenly it blew. High and straight and glorious, the famous *Jet d'Eau* of Geneva, in a great jubilancy of effort, touched the sky for me. I was not disappointed. It was worth waiting for.

JET D'EAU

Touch the sky for me, joyous water,
Show me how earth can reach to heaven
In a single thrust.
Carry me beyond blighted boundary
Of this world's shackled, kerb-stone living.
Heaven's gaiety showered to humankind
In an impulse.

UNWARY SIN

Today the sun is shining,
And there are people in high buildings
With electric lights switched on,
Lights that blink and hum and make a prisoner
    of the day,
Unheeding of the eternal craftsman
Honing summer's way.

God help those poor minions
Trapped in time and space
And shackled by paper contracts and dutifully
    bound
By acts of praise to industry and commerce
    and admin.
While ignorant of the sin,
Committed all unwarily
Of letting God's full gift
Of this fine day, slip,
unjoyfully,
away.

I found the Black Forest deserted and shrouded in early morning mist. There was no sign of habitation, yet even at that hour of the morning a little stall in a lay-by was selling souvenirs, and I stopped to buy one and asked the way to the nearest restaurant. I had a romantic notion of breakfasting in the Black Forest surrounded by trees and birdsong. Well, trees there were, plenty of them, and despite the deserted terrain I at last found a Hansel-and-Gretel-style restaurant with a gingerbread feel to it, and shutters on the windows. But the shutters were closed tight and a sign bore the legend, 'No food until 9 o'clock'.

Walking around the building I found an unshuttered window and could see the proprietor working in the kitchen. 'I've come for breakfast,' I announced, with accompanying sign language. He came to the window and pointed to the poster, 'Not until 9 o'clock'. I struggled quickly to the car and brought him my map and my GB sticker. Tracing the route I had travelled from Brussels to Vienna and back, I stabbed my finger at Luxembourg and explained how I needed to get there today. 'Please let me buy breakfast,' I pleaded, showing him my purse to assure him I was not looking for a handout. He was still not smiling. 'On my way home now,' I said. He turned toward the sink to continue his washing. '*Home*,' I shouted, 'Belfast', and stuck the map under his nose, jabbing my forefinger at Northern Ireland. He looked around and his eyes lit up, 'Ah,' he said, 'Irish, *Irish!*' 'Belfast,' I repeated with a grin, 'Northern Irish.' 'Ja, Ja,' he was smiling now and guiding me into the dining-room, 'come, eat, eat,' he invited. Then his face clouded over again. 'No other food,' he said, indicating the almost empty glass counter in the dining-room. 'Too early.' 'That's OK,' I assured him, 'I'll have whatever is here.' I gazed through the glass at the few dishes of sweets and puddings left and my eyes rested on a luscious looking Black Forest gateau. 'Gateau,' I nodded, pointing, 'I'll have that.' His eyes widened, 'Breakfast?' he queried. 'This for breakfast?' 'Why not?' I chirped. 'I am in the Black Forest after all. What better delicacy to enjoy?' He shook his head in wonder, but went to get a knife to cut me a piece.

The dining-room was large and oblong with wooden tables and benches, and above my head a gallery of wooden slats ran around all four sides of the room. I sat at the table slowly savouring the sweet sickly calories of the gateau, washed down by a huge mug of tea, believing myself to be alone, until a stifled giggle from behind made me turn around and look upwards to the gallery. There, in a straight row, arranged neatly as if for hanging on the washing line, stood a number of striped pyjamas and small night-dresses, all with accompanying bare feet and toes sticking through the wooden slats and wiggling in glee to see this strange wee woman scoffing Black Forest gateau for breakfast. The heads and eyes belonging to the assembled group could barely be seen above the rail, but peered at jaunty angles through the slats. I was about to meet the natives.

Down they came tumbling, hooting, pointing, probing, all talking at once, and there I was, not understanding a word that was said. We laughed a lot, and giggled a great deal, and I mimed and told stories, in my own style of non-verbal communication, and they wanted a taste of the gateau, and I shared it with everyone and had little left to show for my visit.

As I hugged the children goodbye, they responded in an unrestrained manner, reputedly uncharacteristic of their nationality, each one looking deep into my face, until I realised a communication had taken place between us that would have been hard to describe in mere words. The child in me had spoken to the child in them, and who needs words for that?

BE FILLED

Come dine with me, says the Lord of the
    Covenant,
Come take your seat with the children
    of mirth,
Cover the table with trust as an offering,
Breathe my aroma, drink milk of new birth,
      Come gently,
      Come fearless,
      Bring wonder,
      Reap hope,
Unconsciously tasting innocent laughter.
Weigh joy on the scales and measure its worth.
See how you breakfast within Kingdom's
    shadow,
Echoes of whisper from Moses to John,
Let the wild honey wash sand from your
    swallow,
Cup now your hands, catch liquid from rock.
      Come quickly,
      Come often,
      Step lightly,
      Risk heart.
Unconsciously stumbling to Kingdom's edge,
Strain not to feast, suffer love as your pledge.

By mid-afternoon the car wasn't pulling well, I was still about seven miles from Strasbourg and had long since given up all hope of getting to Luxembourg by evening, when it happened. I had just turned off the motorway on to a B-road to Strasbourg when the car packed in. It had already stopped a few times on the way but, after a rest each time, had started again. This time, nothing would induce it to move. I was stuck again – kaput!

For an hour I sat by the roadside praying. No one came to my assistance. In desperation I flagged down a passing motorist but he could not help. 'Why are you making me wait, this time, Lord?' I queried, remembering how he had come to my aid on every previous occasion. Unknown to me, God had more in mind than the fixing of the car. He was about to bring into my life a married couple who were to become firm friends and continued as pen-pals for many years afterwards. Their car stopped and they offered help.

The man could not speak English, but the lady spoke it fluently. Immediately I knew I was safe in their hands. They drove me to a garage, first to get petrol – although I did not believe this was the problem and it proved not to be. My rescuers, who were rapidly proving themselves to be kindred spirits, would not leave me. They worked on the car and got it started and I followed them back to the garage where I discovered that history was about to repeat itself. Again the oil-cap had worked loose and oil had spilt all through the engine. I could not believe that such a thing could happen twice. I was horrified, but fortunately the problem had been diagnosed early enough to attempt a remedy. I thanked the Lord for permitting this minor breakdown in order to prevent a much greater catastrophe. Often he allows an inconvenience in order to prevent a disaster.

My two ministering angels did not abandon me. They knew of another garage in Kehl which would help me at a reasonable cost. Driving ahead, they led me to the place and kept me company while my engine was washed clean and repaired. Then they got me started, despite a flat battery which I would have to get charged the next day. This time my two friends led me to a lovely youth hostel in Kehl where I was able to book a room for the night. God had obviously made me wait a long time by the road-side until these folk arrived, people who were prepared to go the extra mile. It reminded me that when we seem becalmed or stranded, there is always a reason for the delay. Pray without ceasing, as Paul tells us – yes but also with great patience to wait for the answer, as long as it takes for the very best possible answer to come. God doesn't believe in answering with second best.

The following day the drive from Strasbourg to Nancy was pretty painful. Top speed was 45 mph, and even at that I was forcing it. The car could not have done more. It was labouring all the way and I could hear the tell-tale noises of imminent breakdown as we approached the outskirts of Nancy. Unfortunately, these sounds were becoming all too familiar to me. I prayed hard as I strained forward over the steering wheel, 'Please, God, I can't afford to lose any more days – my time is running out. Please don't let me be stranded for hours.' One last cough and a hiccup and Daffe gave up the ghost – where? Right outside a police station.

The gendarmes did not speak English. It was time

for my school-girl French again, and lots of frantic arms flying everywhere. They phoned a garage, and two mechanics came out and worked on the car, giving it its third oil-fill in two days. Something was definitely wrong with my brand-new, second-hand reconditioned engine which had cost me dearly, and had been guaranteed to last some considerable time.

The gendarmes insisted that I drive to the nearest hotel, which was far beyond my price-range. I begged to be shown to a camp-site, but apparently it was a long distance away, and I did not want to risk forcing the vehicle further, especially since it refused to budge from the main street outside this hotel. My police friends insisted that I would be arrested if I let it sit there. So they had to push me around the corner where it could legally park until the morning.

There I was, stuck for the night, handing over my last remaining French francs to a rather curt lady who insisted she would require more but would put up with it. I was not able, therefore, to afford the cost of a drink of orange at the end of a day during which I had seen no food or drink since breakfast. I was thirsty beyond all my previous experiences of drought, and begged for a cup of tea. She declared that she didn't serve tea, in a tone of voice which suggested that I had just asked for arsenic. Fanta was now too expensive for me. She said I could have water or wine. I explained that I was a teetotaller, and I was afraid that the drinking of water in France would inevitably place me as a hostage to the bathroom for the foreseeable future – for days, perhaps even for weeks. She was not amused, nor did she bend an inch.

I went to bed with no money, no food, no transport, and my tongue hanging out of my mouth like a rusty nail from a sandpapered washboard. I was at my lowest ebb, and all I could find in my provisions was a packet of ready-salted crisps. It was like eating chips of granite on a trek across the Sahara Desert. Thinking back, I felt as if I lay in a gravel pit all night, turning and twisting on serrated edges of heat exhaustion and dehydration. My headache got worse and worse, passing far beyond the pain-barrier, and my tongue was so swollen in my mouth that I could not even cry without giving it a nasty bite. By 3 a.m. I decided to get up and spend the night in prayer in order to take control of the high temperature and feelings of deep despondency which were threatening to swamp me.

REMEMBER

Remind me of your promise, Lord
    Jesus Christ,
Embrace me in your arms and hold me firm,
Please lead me to cool pools where David
    bathed,
I shall not want.
Strength for the hardest task, you
    promised me,
Guidance to navigate the darkest night,
Why does it feel I'll never reach the dawn?
Stay by my side.

Can you not wait one night with me, my little
    one?
I'll never leave you, child, that's what I said.
Then walk with me down corridors of fear,
Beyond is light.

But, Father God, I'm scared to round another
  corner,
What if there be dragons at earth's dark end?
And me upon a course towards dragon's
  breath?
I dare not look.

Dragons, certainly my child, and much more
  besides,
But long before poor dragons walked the
  earth,
Can you recall what wondrous things I did,
With Holy Fire?

The morning had not so much dawned as shuddered into view. By 8.30 a.m. I had struggled back to the car, without breakfast of course, as I had no French francs left. My thirst was now exacerbated far beyond toleration levels. I don't suppose the French Foreign legion would ever accept me as a volunteer (too short), however, if they ever thought about it, they might find I have had considerable experience in withstanding the rigors of desert conditions despite the fact that I have never been in your actual Sahara. But then deserts come in all shapes and concepts, don't they? – especially for those struggling to learn discipleship. Thanks to God's grace, I had withstood the night, but I badly needed some liquid. 'Where, Lord?' I pleaded. 'How? I have no more cash!'

By now I should have been safely back on British soil and shopping in Sainsbury's or Tesco. In my mind a thought broke through sharply: 'Search the boot again.' 'What?' I thought. 'Search a boot I knew was empty? Why?' But out I got and dragged myself without expectation to the rear of the car. I ran my fingers unenthusiastically through the pile of empty crisp bags and discarded biscuit wrappings, in the picnic basket. From the torn remainder of a packet fell one single Rich Tea biscuit and I grabbed it like a crazed vulture. It slipped from my grasp and I nearly fell headlong into the boot in my attempt to rescue it before it hit the grubby floor. As I shot my hand out to regain my balance the palm staved itself down and into the empty cavern which should have held my spare wheel secure. The same spare wheel which the garage in Luxembourg had forgotten to replace on the outward journey.

I winced at the stab of pain in my wrist and then forgot the pain instantly as my fingers, groping for a better grip to reinstate myself vertically, collided with a round, tubby object, still miraculously cool, hidden away in its dark cocoon. Arthur extracting Excalibur from its ancient sheath could not have given such an incredible whoop of joy as I emitted when my right hand pulled into view the most welcome tin of Fanta I had ever seen in my life. It was cold, and it was full.

Tears of joy flooded down my face as I sat balanced precariously on the boot in full view of a score of luxury, five-star hotels, noisily scoffing my breakfast of Fanta and a single Rich Tea biscuit. The clientele, observing as they reclined with hot croissants and coffee, while dripping jewelled charm-bracelets in the strawberry preserve, may well have wondered at the sight of such obvious Dickensian deprivation being relieved, rather too hastily for the good of my digestion. As for me, I could not have dined more right-royally if it had been the Ritz. I raised my tin to the five-star lounge window and shouted loudly into the empty street, 'Thank you Lord – Mercy.' And the gassy response produced by my gobbled Fanta, cheerily burped, 'Amen.'

Now the big question was, would the car start? I prayed silently, as I twisted my hand clockwise on the ignition key – and what a relief when, without complaint, the engine clattered into life. I set off with a grateful heart on the remaining short two-hour journey to Luxembourg. The car was severely labouring, though, and I limped along with smoke pouring out behind.

My old friends in the convent gave me a wonderful welcome back, and I was treated to a feast. But the best part was the milk – actual cow's milk, cold and thick, and as much as I could drink.

That night I dreamt while I slept. It was a wonderful dream of lying down the next night in a British bed, on British soil again. When I woke up it seemed more incredible than a fairy-tale. Considering what had yet to be done this day in Luxembourg, and the miles still to be journeyed, the vision of the dream appeared so remote and unobtainable that I put it down to wishful thinking. Rising at 6 a.m. I enjoyed a sumptuous breakfast before making my way, in trepidation, to the British Embassy.

The smiling face and generous hug that greeted me at the Embassy was Maddy's welcome. It was a great reunion and she phoned the garage and explained the situation. They admitted having the wheel and said to bring the car round as it should not be in difficulty.

It broke down again between leaving the Embassy and arriving at the garage and I had to phone them to come and get me. Despite this, and the fact that the mechanic had to work on it for some considerable time to get it started again, I was informed, on arrival, that there was little wrong with the engine. My spare wheel was reinstated in the boot and another mechanic tinkered some more, but they were obviously quite eager to bid me farewell. I was instructed that I must keep filling the car with oil every hundred miles or so for a couple of months before the engine would 'settle' because it was only a second-hand one. I thought this sounded rather odd. As you can imagine, my feelings on leaving Luxembourg were mixed.

Two more delays caused by oil leakage left me hardly daring to dream that I might make the ferry. But at 6.15 p.m. I was driving into Ostend and, for the first time for a while now, was not late for a boat.

THE HOME STRAIGHT

Maybe I'll be back one day
To share with Good Samaritans
Who went that extra mile to pave my way.
Or see them next when, at the judgement
    gate,
We each arrive to pay the bill
For all the bridges that we crossed
Forgetting we must pay the cost,
For every route we wander off the way,
And there he'll stand, the keeper of the gate,
And maybe he'll be laughing as I stumble in,
Dishevelled, tired and late,
And as he pays my entrance with his credit
I'll see the line of people marching through
Who paved the way, to oil my path, and pay
    my due.

5 BY ROYAL INVITATION

London – Buckingham Palace

London, an old friend from many adventures past, could hardly be described as a novelty where I was concerned. But this time was certainly different. To be able to drive on through one of the front gates of Buckingham Palace with a wave and a welcome and an official invitation to the summer Garden Party in my pocket – this was novelty alright.

It was July 1981: Monica Wilson and I had been invited to the Garden Party in recognition of the work done in Northern Ireland for the International Year of Disabled People. Each guest had been allowed to bring an escort and I naturally did not need to think twice about who that should be – which explains why my Mum was sitting there white-knuckled, braving the London rush-hour traffic. We were all dressed up to the nines and looking the part as we drove up the Mall, feeling really special alongside all the taxis, Rolls and Jags heading for the Palace.

The police waved us through the gate to the sound of a clatter of tourist cameras as they strained to get a photo of us. Did they think we were important? Well, maybe just for a day, we were. Once on foot Mum and I were directed through a side archway and out onto the main lawn at the back of the Palace.

Although there were hundreds of people present, an air of relaxed anticipation prevailed and folk wandered chatting and sipping tea as if they were quite used to passing the odd afternoon like this whenever the notion took them. Eager footmen kept materialising on every side, and at every possible opportunity, to dance attendance on needs we didn't know we had. I began to see what it must be like to be royalty.

As it was high summer, the 'style' was much in evidence. Lovely billowy, floaty creations of fragile material wafted by on the cucumber trail of neat little crustless sandwiches, and there seemed to be almost more hats than people, or maybe they were just larger than the people. I had chosen to wear a relatively flimsy, heart-necklined, pastel pink catsuit with matching jacket, each edged with fine pearls embroidered into the neck of both bodice and jacket. Then the heavens opened and the tropical storm of the previous day decided to give an encore. Everything got soaked including the tiny crescent-shaped hat of leaves which I had soldered to the back of my head with strategically-placed clips. Mum and I beat a hasty retreat to the Pavilion for shelter and to enjoy afternoon tea. It was set out beautifully with a delicious exuberance of savouries: little patties and salmon vol-au-vents and tiny pancakes that could be balanced on a finger-tip. Not to mention the sweets: three-layered gateaux with two layers of cream, and the flavours: chocolate, vanilla, lemon, with icing unparalleled, and the customary strawberries and cream, plus raspberries and cream and any amount of other combinations of cakes and pastries and fruits – all a gourmet could desire – and all with cream. It was just as well that we had been warned not to lunch before arrival because, by the time the Queen was announced at 4 p.m., the assembled guests had well and truly eaten.

On the hour precisely she descended the long, sweeping steps to the lawn. At 3.45 p.m. the rain had stopped and everyone had gone wandering a little further afield down to the lake to see the flamingos. As this seemed quite a stretch for me to walk, Mum and I had given it a miss and instead queued early to see the Queen. We did not regret it.

Parallel lines had formed, winding down and round the lawn, and we had an unbroken view of the Palace terrace as the beefeaters led the royal party down the steps towards us. The Queen came first with Prince Philip, then Princess Anne, Princess Alexandra and ... who was that coming behind? Was it ... ? An excited buzz ran around the assembled crowd as they spotted who was bringing up the rear. Only six days before their wedding, Prince Charles and Lady Diana, as she was then, had decided to attend as well.

I was in the very front of my line, with Mum standing behind me, and, as Prince Philip halted fleetingly at the foot of the steps and then turned to walk along the line parallel to my own, I realised what was about to happen. The royal party divided, each to opposite lines, but the Queen kept walking forward until she stopped in front of me.

Her Majesty held out a gloved hand and enquired where I had come from. She was the concerned hostess, even apologising for the weather, as if anyone could have altered that. I especially appreciated her thoughtfulness when, at the end of our conversation, instead of moving along the line, she took the trouble to reach her hand behind me to Mum with the words, 'You must be Hilary's mother?' Since the lines were, by now, three tiers deep, our hostess might have saved herself some time by addressing only the front row, but Mum was not left out.

Diana came next, to a flurry of excited questions about the royal wedding. As she stopped in front of me she pulled off her left glove and pushed her hand on to my palm with the words, 'Would you like to see my ring?' It was a spontaneous act of natural exuberance. Then I was officially presented to Princess Anne who took a prolonged interest in the full-length musical which we had written and produced for the International Year of Disabled People, and she seemed to have been well-briefed as to all the details. By the time Prince Charles was moving up the line, the rain had turned into a deluge, and I was attempting to hold my umbrella over a Scottish gentleman sitting in a wheelchair beside me, his smart suit getting more soggy by the minute. The two of us had enjoyed good conversation as we waited, and as I was intent on my brolly service I did not see the approaching Prince until I looked up to find him smiling down at me somewhat bemused to have taken me by surprise. 'Do you two know each other?' he asked with a grin. 'We do now!' was the united reply from the young man and myself and all three – Scot, Ulsterwoman and Prince – collapsed into laughter. 'I think,' said the Prince, 'there have been many friendships made here today.' He wasn't wrong, and that just about summed up the day for us all.

THE KING

What royal chandelier illuminates a stable?
What edict crowned a carpenter a king?
What truth escaped from Herod's fable?
Who released a million choirs upon the wing?
'Twas love, my Lord,
'Twas only love could do it.

Love in the stature of a God.
Till commoners and statesmen kneel together
In the wayward places of the earth.

What crown can grace a human forehead
More than the pain profound enough to cleanse
  a world?
Crown of thorns that draws the blood of
  saviour
Renders all statesmen dumb, leaves flags still
  furled.
Come Yahweh, Lord and Spirit,
Build your throne in heart and mind and soul,
Till kneeling on your carpet crimson red
The sweet anointing of your sceptre makes us
  whole.

July 1982 wrapped its days into a tight ball and
hurled itself at me with increasing velocity as the
weeks flew past my unguarded goal-posts. On the
long-term agenda the forthcoming holiday month of
August had promised the possibility of relaxation,
with evening meetings at an end – and maybe even a
travel-break salvaged after attendance at an Open
University summer school in Brighton. A leisurely
holiday month, I thought. However, God knew better.
  Studying with the Open University since 1978
had become one of my main hobbies. Some of the
years included a summer school week, and on this
particular course I was registered to attend the
University in Brighton in three weeks' time. But my
psychology studies in July were interrupted when an
exciting confirmation arrived from Stormont Castle
– confirmation that I had been invited to attend
Buckingham Palace for the royal Garden Party for the

second year running. My friends suggested all sorts of reasons for a repeat invitation: 'Perhaps they want you to return the silver,' was one wisecrack, but then, that is what friends are for, isn't it?

Rushing into town in the afternoon, I changed my boat reservations for a sailing several days earlier than would have been necessary for the summer school.

Recently, somewhere in the back of my mind, a madcap notion had been forming. Since my tour across Europe in the car I had always imagined that I would like to try another European drive, north-wards this time, through the Netherlands to Scandinavia. One of my favourite primary-school teachers, Miss Glass, had instilled in me a childhood vision of the fjords in Norway, and I had always longed to visit them some day.

However, I wanted to make sure this was God's will, especially after all the disastrous car break-downs of the last escapade. I decided to wait to see if God opened the doors along the way before com-mitting myself fully to this journey. So I did not pack the necessary equipment to sleep in the car, but at the last moment, I did slip my passport into my luggage just before I sat on top of the case to force the lid shut.

On arrival in England, I 'did' the London shops. Well, if the truth be told, Oxford Street pretty nearly 'did' me. At one stage I found myself resting against the window of a travel agent's and the old familiar, inner tug-nudge which tells me it is no coincidence was there again. In I went and gathered all the information I would need for the Netherlands and Scandinavia, just in case.

Returning to Hyde Park I digested all the material

sitting outside in the sun and feeding the ducks. It was a really happy and peaceful hour-and-a-half which I spent there, enjoying the lake, and the peace had only been broken once when I was startled by a loud bang. My immediate instinct was to run, as it sounded identical to the blasts I was used to hearing at home when a bomb goes off. But I restrained the urge and told myself not to be silly, I was in London now, not Belfast, and it was probably a lunch-time ceremonial salute of some kind, like the 1 p.m. gun at Edinburgh Castle.

Imagine my amazement, on leaving the Park, to find myself stuck in several hours of snarled-up traffic and to hear the car radio announce that two bombs had gone off in London that day, one of them in Hyde Park itself, where I had been enjoying my freedom from Ulster's turmoil. I said a very thankful prayer to the Boss remembering his promise, '. . . and lo I am with you always, to the end of the age' (Matt. 28.20).

It was well into the evening before I managed to crawl my way back to the hotel through the still almost stationary traffic, but I was able to go by way of Leicester Square and buy a ticket for the play *Children of a Lesser God*. I knew I would really enjoy seeing it on Friday evening – and I was not disappointed.

NO LESSER GOD

No lesser God was he
Who stood sentinel at the womb
On the day earth gouged me from the stars,
A speck of dust, sheared clean,
Gleaned from edge of reason,
Mainspring snapped tight against the dying.

No lesser God to stand
From edge to edge of precipice,
As I unwary tread the path of fire.
His loving hands spread wide
To hold the tilt of earth pinched firm
Between both uncut thumbnails of his will.
No lesser God is mine
Who measured out his Kingdom stride
With prime skill of such exactitude
To frame his majesty,
Twinned at cradle and on cross,
He who walked earth's cinders without shoes.

The morning of the Garden Party produced the perfect weather forecast. Bright sunshine throughout and no threat of the torrential rain which had accompanied my first Garden Party at the Palace the previous year. I took my time in preparation, dressing with unhurried glee and, even if I do day so myself, was rather pleased with the result in the mirror. I am sure the little cherub at the top right-hand corner of the shabbily gilded frame winked at me as I turned to go.

As I drove up the Mall I discovered, to my surprise, that many people were already gathered along its full stretch. It was only 12.30 p.m., and yet I was fortunate to find a space close to the top and only 100 yards from the particular Palace gate which I was to enter later.

It was really hot by now, and the sight was wonderful. Large stretches of green grass in St James's Park were covered with families carefully lounging on rugs, and distributing tea and sandwiches gingerly across meticulously ironed knees. Everyone looked as though they had stepped from a Julie Andrews movie and I noticed a distinct absence of sticky buns. Freshly laundered white gloves were waving conspicuously across the grass at each other, and chocolate was not being eaten.

A family on the rug behind invited me to join them for a sandwich and a chat and before I knew where I was it was 1.45 p.m. and time to return to the car to don the Hat. Now this was not going to be as easy as one might suppose, considering that I have a great aversion to wearing hats, on account of the fact that, to do so, usually reduces me to the proportions of a king-sized mushroom with two feet sticking out below. Then I invariably require a periscope to see where I am going in order to avoid collision with lamp-posts and other tall, inanimate objects. On this particular occasion, however, it was a neat little piece of millinery which clung snugly to the back of my head, allowing safe forward navigation. It clung, that is, on days when the temperature was not soaring past perspiration point, and when I did not have to perambulate for long enough for the pendulum swing of my gait to shake it off at every fourth step.

I started the walk to the Palace. By the fourth step the hat was in my hand and stayed there until I was safely inside the hallowed precincts of the royal loo and could do an anchor job with hair-clips and spittle. That little mirror cherub had probably stopped winking now and was chuckling disgracefully.

Refreshed and freshly groomed, I stepped out onto the lawn and took in the sight of that large crowd of guests promenading in the elegance and style of the occasion. This year, with no rain, the little tables had been arranged outside the grand marquees and the whole atmosphere was a cross between a day at the fair and the film-set of a Jane Austen novel.

As I began to descend the steps towards the lawn, a nearby gentleman in a beefeater costume rushed over and offered his arm. I was, by now, beginning to feel a little like Alice in the Looking Glass. We chatted as we descended and, having discovered that I was a Deaconess, he insisted that I come with him to be introduced to someone who would be particularly happy to meet me.

The elderly gentleman was seated with his wife at a table with an African diplomat and his wife, who was dressed in a very bright and decorative costume but was unable to speak much English. Since making conversation has never been my particular problem, the Englishman's wife and I were soon engrossed in chat. She was a friendly soul and we got on well. As her husband was wearing a dog-collar I had no queries as to why my escort had introduced us and I leant over to include him in our conversation. 'Is your parish a big one?' I asked.

Well, it seemed like a reasonable enough enquiry to me, so why were his eyes twinkling with merriment, and why was she suppressing a smile? 'Large enough,' he replied enigmatically. I tried again. 'Is it far from here?' 'It's in the neighbourhood,' he smiled as he sipped his tea. The conversation continued like this for some time before his wife could suppress her laughter no longer and insisted that her husband confess the truth. He then disclosed, with genial humour, that he was one of the private chaplains to the Queen. It was a privilege to talk shop with him.

When the Queen arrived it was different from the previous year. This time she did not walk along lines of folk, stopping to chat at will, but restricted her progress to a central corridor where individuals had already been chosen for presentation. Fortunately I found myself right at the front of the top, short end of the open three-sided rectangular shape of people queuing to catch a glimpse of the royal party. As the Queen moved forward, this short line was able to move slowly in her wake, which meant she was in clear view the whole time and only an arm's length away for over an hour. The Duke of Edinburgh came round to my side and kept me in good company and chat for some of the way. Even Prince Charles noticed my marathon walk and carried my plate of tea and pastries to my table at the end of the parade, insisting that I saw the lake and glorious flower gardens before I left. I tried to go as far as Princess Anne's doll's house, but the old legs had done enough and I contented myself with gateau and ice-cream on the lawn. I felt like Winnie the Pooh, or was it Paddington Bear, licking my fingers daintily, and well out of sight of my esteemed hosts, and musing on how this had definitely been a right, royal day.

6 NORTH TO THE FJORDS

Holland – Denmark – Sweden – Norway

On my last day in London I prayed for guidance to find the AA place, if God meant me to make further enquiries about Scandinavia. The answer to prayer came, as I drove into Leicester Square in search of a Midland Bank, and there, right next door, hung the big black and yellow sign, proclaiming AA as loudly as I desired. The AA official took endless trouble making all the relevant enquiries on my behalf, and encouraged me as regards the possibilities for the journey. I had been watching so carefully for even the slightest hint of a slamming door; instead all the windows seemed to be flying open in every direction. Nevertheless, I was determined to wait and see how things were after the summer school before making the final decision about the tour.

The week at the OU summer school flew past in an endless stream of lectures, projects, and assignments. Afterwards I drove back to London, effortlessly, and was in Leicester Square by 10 a.m. sitting on a tall stool in the AA office and praying that arrangements would not be possible if this was not God's will. Everything just seemed to slot into place at an almost alarming rate, right down to the fact that I got the very last place on the boat for that evening. It was too much of a coincidence: I knew I had to go.

In the afternoon I drove to Sheerness, stopping

95

only to stock up on films for my cameras and food for the three-week adventure ahead.

Several frantic phone calls home confirmed that the trip was on. I thanked God for the understanding of my family: my mother, who had been half-prepared for me charging off on another mad-cap journey, was not averse to the idea, although I could hear the nervousness in her voice as she bade me goodbye on the telephone.

I enjoyed the sail to Holland and found the Dutch people to be one of the most friendly groups I had yet encountered – a nation of kindred spirits to my own temperament – and I quickly felt very much at home. Without equipment or furnishings for sleeping in the car, I was resigned to the cost of b&b accommodation throughout this trip, and spent a great deal of time that day finding and queuing at the tourist information office, which finally found me a lovely place to stay with a typical little Continental café across the street, complete with outdoor tables and umbrellas, where I was able to sit sipping tea in the cool of the evening, lifting my cup to toast the Boss and thank him for getting me safely on foreign soil.

The next day I discovered the joys of Amsterdam, sailing along the canals in a glass-bottomed boat, buying beautiful posters in the quaint art shops, and an afternoon exploring the Floriada where a person can wander forever through the glorious flower gardens and lakes, making friends on the way.

I enjoyed quiet, unspectacular driving the next day, through the homely Dutch farmlands to Hengelo, with the comforting repetition of cattle and farmsteads to ease my progress. There was something cosy about this little town, more than the big city. It felt civilised and sensible, and as I had driven enough for one day, I surrendered to its refined allure and relaxed for two nights here in a lovely hotel – with real strawberries for breakfast. Not only that, but the buffet table groaned with bowls of every fruit imaginable – in addition to ham, meat, cheese and a number of items I couldn't even identify.

The heat that evening and the following day was unbearable, rising to 32 degrees centigrade. Here I was able to drink two pints of milk without a single stare from the locals, before a long chat with the Boss at the fountain at Almelo and an early night to catch up on my lost sleep.

The next morning, I gained the wrong impression as regards distances from the maps, and did not make it to the ferry-crossing to Denmark that night. So, changing my money into German marks, I stayed in a motel on the motorway this side of Hamburg. The following morning took me from Hamburg to Puttgarden and then I caught the boat to Rødbyhavn in Denmark. It was not a cheap voyage but a lovely trip in brilliant sunshine – until the Baltic Sea decided to treat me to its mixed idiosyncrasies of haze and mistiness, but, for an addictive sailor like myself, it was all part of the cruise.

From there to Copenhagen, and time well-spent in the Central Station securing a hotel. If I had been aware of the city's notoriously high incidence of theft, especially with regard to tourists, I might have held my handbag a little tighter as I stood in line with the long string of back-packers queuing at the station for b&b accommodation. It was a few days later that I came face to face with a living statistic of this problem, and encountered his pain.

In the mean time I spent Saturday seeing the

tourist attractions, shopping – well, window-shopping; at Copenhagen's prices, that was about as much as I could afford – and then to the famous Tivoli Pleasure Gardens. It would give entirely the wrong impression of the place to call it an amusement park. There were amusements, lots of them, but discreetly positioned.

The real beauty of the place was the lake, stretching for what seemed like miles, and lit at night in a thousand colours and shapes of celebration. Little illuminated, open-air restaurants bedecked its shores and were built out onto the water like tempting titbits to inveigle the wildfowl that graced its circumference. With two open-air theatres, juggling and circus-type buskers everywhere, vying with traditional pantomime acts, it was not surprising that I stayed for seven hours and did not notice the time passing. As I crawled late to bed that night, the visual images of amazing tubes of tumbling water and cascading fountains lulled me to sleep. Like the song says, I was glad to be in 'Wonderful Copenhagen'.

COPENHAGEN

World-famous and beckoning, the Gardens
    dazzled,
Their lights bouncing in the gathering dusk,
Promising Christmas in July.
Circus and pantomime belying calendar
    dictation,
Solidifying time in chronicles of celebration,
Memos to make our own allegiance with
    life's commemoration.

Lake rippled, and vibrating, my fancy
rested,
Free of deadlines, no hostage towards the
morrow.
Embracing this day in the now.
Flying swans, jostling the crowd,
Their wings beating airsongs towards
encounter,
The created animation – loud, pale shadows
of creator.

It was Sunday and my rest-day. I was delighted to
find a church in the same street as my hotel. Having
gone to the door of the church very early I sat on a
stone outside awaiting entry, and a man began to walk
up the pathway toward the door. Unshaven, with his
clothes well-creased and dishevelled, the stranger
looked more than a little scruffy. He began to speak
to me and I responded cautiously, measuring the distance to the car in carefully calculated glances, in
case an attempt at a hasty retreat would be necessary.

Despite his unkempt appearance, his voice was
refined and his excellent English was used in a
manner that suggested an educated mind and a good
upbringing. He said he was a French-Canadian, a
chaplain to the Forces now working in Germany. His
poor appearance, he said, was due to the fact that,
while in the station the previous day, all his luggage
had been stolen and, because it was the weekend, no
one could help. The police had assisted a little, but
had explained that the high number of incidents of this
kind in the city, in the peak holiday season, did not
augur well for any hope of retrieving his belongings,

and they had sent him to his country's embassy. Unfortunately it had been shut for the weekend and he had to wait until Monday before trying again. I do not know where he had spent the previous night but, by the look of him, it couldn't have been too comfortable.

All my instincts of self-protection warned me against automatically assuming this story to be factual – and yet something in the man's eyes confirmed for me that he was sincere. What was I to do? I remembered the many times in the past when God had brought human angels of mercy to minister to me when I was in trouble during my travels. Now here was the possibility of a fellow-traveller needing my help. I knew I could not refuse if his predicament was genuine – but if it wasn't, and I was wrong? It was quite a dilemma.

I invited him to come into the service with me and speak to the minister at its conclusion. This would at least give me time to observe his behaviour during worship and help to ascertain if he really was a chaplain or not. At the end of worship I was more convinced than ever of his genuine plight and strongly aware of the Lord's bidding, but the local minister seemed unimpressed with his story and gave him only 60 crowns, not nearly enough for a b&b for the night, let alone food to last the day. The man looked hungrily at the pittance the minister had pressed into his hand, smiled a hearty thanks at me, and moved towards the door, waving goodbye to me as he left.

I said a fervent prayer to the Boss that I was not making a mistake: 'If I'm right, Lord,' I prayed, 'I cannot refuse to be an answer to his prayer for help. And if I'm wrong, please protect me from all evil, for I do this for all the right reasons.' Then I moved after him as quickly as I could and offered my help.

We stayed together all morning. I drove him to the beach and spread a picnic rug on the sands. Opening the boot of the car I emptied the contents of my food stores onto the rug without discrimination or selection. He was starving by this time, not having eaten since early the previous day. As I watched him tuck hungrily into the humble lunch of rolls and crisps and tins of meat and fruit, I couldn't help thinking of the wee boy with the loaves and fishes who had unreservedly allowed Jesus to take them and feed the hungry crowds.

I felt the joy of seeing the hungry fed and knew the thrill of being able to return even a small portion of all the help and care I had received at the hands of strangers through the years. He went to book a hotel for the night with 80 crowns more, and a brand-new toothbrush and tube of toothpaste. I thought that was the last I would hear from the wayfarer. But, true to his word, when I arrived home at the end of the holiday, there was a letter waiting for me – a letter of Christian gratitude, with photographs of his whole family. He was dressed in the full clerical garb of a Forces chaplain. For a long time afterwards he sent me postcards from the many exotic countries of his subsequent travels. I look forward to meeting him again in heaven.

LOAVES AND FISHES

It's only five, Lord,
Just five loaves
And they're so small.
Small as the strength which brought me here
Squandered in the effort of the climb.
Was it worth it Lord?
To come so far?

When five thousand heads of crowd block you
    from view?
And I can hardly hear the words you teach
From the pounding in my ears,
From the aching of my feet,
Hope dissipated by the effort of the climb.
Let me rest here, upon the grass,
And eat the fishes in my bag.
There are only five, Lord,
Just five little spricks*
And very small.
Perhaps someone in this vast crowd
Will tell me later what you said,
And how you spoke with such authority
And I can go back home
And tell the tale.

Tell how I didn't see the master's face,
Five thousand people blocked it out from view,
But at least I'd know that I had made the climb,
And sat cross-legged upon the grass
With all the other pilgrims,
I could believe, within a mile of him.
Then I looked up and, here, a man
Was stooping at my side,
Was reaching out his hand,
Was asking me for food.
But five small loaves
And just as many fishes,
Surely you don't ask a little one to share?
He smiled and brought me to his friend,
A master worthy of the name,
And when I looked into his face,

*An Ulster word for a tiny fish.

I knew why the climb had been so hard
And why it was I came.
And as he took the five and five into his hands,
Big palms they were that easily held together
That which was meant as picnic just for me,
I lifted up my head to see the starving crowd
And in that second saw them fed,
And in that glimpse saw thousands more,
And in that wave of pain and joy,
Heard multitudes with anguish roar.

In the afternoon I found the famous Little Mermaid statue and sat beside her, quietly resting and praying for all strangers on their complex journeys far from home.

The sail across the narrow strait was short but took me into the first bad weather I had seen since leaving Britain. Damp mizzle reminded me how far North I had come. In the wet dankness the official gave my car a full search and made me wait some considerable time alone in a small room. Feeling like a criminal, I huddled in the dank, utilitarian waiting-room preparing to answer the blunt questions regarding Belfast and the reasons for my journey for the umpteenth time. As the afternoon wore on, I began to wonder what a cell in Sweden was like and would I have to spend the night in one? Fortunately, that was not necessary and my passport was returned in time for me to find a motel for the night.

The officer turned up at the motel the next morning to make sure I was directed safely on my way to Norway. I never did discover what they were looking for. But fellow guests at my hotel told me horror stories of the drug-trafficking route from Holland to Scandinavia, and the ruthless smugglers who travel

103

it. I didn't think I looked anything like a ruthless smuggler, but apparently they used exactly the same route which I had taken in my journey to date.

Feeling somewhat like an escaped prisoner, I proceeded with a certain amount of haste towards the Norwegian border.

Prices in both Norway and Sweden were much higher than elsewhere on this trip, but Oslo gifted me with grand buildings and pretty fountains and something else – a warm welcome to strangers from the locals, which made me feel that I had again come to a country where I could stay awhile.

I arose the next day to temperatures akin to home, but a brightness and clarity in the air which lightened my step. The next objective, and the main one for this trip, was the fjords. All day I drove and was amazed at how much the scenery mirrored both Scotland, and Donegal. I knew that the journey was about 240 miles but that it might take longer than I had anticipated due to the terrain. I wasn't wrong.

By tea-time, I was in the fjords, and I do mean *in* them – great jagged mountains, towering and threatening to squeeze me to pulp in the narrow little slits of gullies between. The road – one-track, with hairpin bends which whipped round mercilessly to catch the unsuspecting driver unawares from before and behind – balanced precariously on the very edge of a precipice.

My entrance to the fjords was so sudden it took me unawares. From a flat road I turned a corner and hovered momentarily on the top of searing cliffs to the left, to the right and underneath my car, plunging their sides with knife-edged precision to the gully floor, too far down for me to see. Not one to be in any way afraid of heights, I nevertheless experienced an unprecedented lurch of the stomach as I began the descent, at an angle frighteningly close to the perpendicular, uncertain of my ability to stop. Round and round, and down and round I hurtled, on God's humorous thumbing of the nose at man's pathetic attempts at constructing a Big Dipper. No amusement park had ever made my heart pound like this – but I was totally unprepared for the tunnels.

The first one came at me like a charging bull. I had just rounded a bend on a one-track pathway, close to a cliff-edge drop, and suddenly I was plunged into pitch darkness. The blackness swallowed me completely. There wasn't even time to see it coming. Now I understood why the locals seemed to keep their headlights dipped at all times in daylight, even in summer. I resisted the urge to ram on the brakes as I was frightened of skidding in the dank cave-like atmosphere, and prayed that any other vehicle in the tunnel with me would at least have its lights on. My hand shot to my own light switch and dispelled the awful blackness. This first tunnel felt like a mile long, and it took me all of that time to regain my composure from the sudden shock. All around and above me was solid rock and I realised that, until then, I had never really experienced pitch blackness in its devastation.

ROCK SOLID

Raven-winged with pitch, the black engulfed
    me,
Jonah-like I floundered in the belly of the dark.
More shocked than fearful, I struggled for
    a light,
This darkness had no end.

Then came the fear, fear that knows
    redundancy of senses,
Eyes that cannot see, stare in agonising
    helplessness,
Without clues of height or depth, lock on to
    nothingness.
Frozen stare on Paul's Damascus road.
Delegating trust to other senses.
All outer sense is stilled, inner life takes
    mastery.
The car, newly discovered chrysalis, held me
    bound
As it journeyed through the vacuum and I
    began to feel,
To sense, the walls about me, touch the roof
    above
With unknown sense long-stilled.

Caverns too black to see,
Burgeoned with womb-dark rememberings,
I'd been here before, before sense was mine
    to use.
Alive, yet unborn, I had traversed this journey
In the midnight of my birth,
Rejected from the womb in baptism of fire,
Welcomed by unremitting pain.
Before I was mistress of the spoken word,
My only knowledge then was feeling,
And now, here, I was entombed to feel again.

Unspoken was the cry that fired itself from
    earth to heaven,
Quicksilver was its speed to Father God.
Too gripped tight with fear to speak,

I reached for him who is the Word.
And then I knew the fragility of darkness.
How it shifts and stretches thin,
Now a mere veil-torn consistency
When that which is more solid enters in.
Walls, roof and floor of this pinched orifice,
Were no enemy but friend,
For he who calls himself the Rock
Has hacked through every cleft of Hell
And engineered each tunnel's end.
I knew for sure it was not darkness
That had embraced my soul from birth to
    death,
Caught between the seeing and the blindness.
Looking now to caverns' sides with eyes of
    faith,
Remembering then, what swallowed me was
    solid Rock.

Bergen welcomed me in capital fashion. From this smart and stylish city ships leave regularly for all points north, south, east and west. I had wondered if I might visit Iceland before returning home, but the weather and the time it would have taken to add this project to the journey militated against going further. I booked a ticket home to the UK and, after several restful days here, found myself once again at the docks homeward bound.

DOCK-LANDS

I've watched the sun set on a thousand of
    earth's dock-lands,
I've seen the sun go down in the dockyards
    of the world.
I've smelt the fragrance of Belfast in each
    harbour's greasy mix,
The air of fish-kill, putrid on each harbour's
    concrete beach,
I've reeled in the cry of sea birds,
Staunched life-cycle's flow of weeping,
Knowing that, wherever voyagers travel,
The gulls forever call.
And when I stand in stasis,
Haunted by allure of water,
I'll admit the dock-lands to the ingress of
    my soul.

Stand with me on dock-lands, herons of
    the world.
For all of them are beautiful,
And all of them are terrible,
The ugliness of being each the same.
I'll stay upon the quayside,
To the rancour of your chains,
Pledging to my master the freedom, now
    to be
Standing on the dock-land, going home.

7 ITALY REACHED AT LAST

Belgium – France – Switzerland –
Italy – the Rivieras

The restlessness that is not discontent is what drives me out to seek new sights and fresh sounds. Both blessed and cursed is the dynamism of the yearning for strange smells and the touch of a breeze smelted from the heat of a Continental forest or dredged from the depths of a Mediterranean lake. The fire in the belly need not be a crude, earth-bound stab at gratification, but a lifting beyond to experience a satisfaction that was both designed for, and subsequently lost in, the Garden of Eden. At the anvil of God's making we accept our passions and our drives. He will fashion them into beauty if we submit to him and relinquish their ugliness to the forging of his will.

I was driven by heart and mind to go walkabout again. My first tour across the Continent had been much shorter than I had intended because of the disastrous car breakdown, and I had not reached Italy. I wanted to prove to myself that I could return to these lands without breakdowns, and I very much wished to visit Italy to complete my sense of unfinished business with Europe.

It had been 11 years since that first fateful journey, and I had prayed, during all that time, for the guidance and the courage to try again. The possibility opened up when I was given the opportunity to represent our Northern Ireland Deaconess Association at the World Conference of Diakonia in Berne, Switzerland, in July 1987.

Settling for an overnight stop in Versailles, I found myself camping beside a bright orange van which housed a South African couple. We shared about our respective countries, and the learning and the companionship which resulted made it evident why God had led me to spend time at this venue.

COLOUR CODING

Camp-fires and conversation,
Cauldron of contemplation,
Sanctify vision,
As severed world's touch.
Liberation from tides unknown,
Tongued by a hurt unshorn,
Knife to the lamb's wool,
Feel heart's sacrifice.

Hearing your turmoil,
I echo your tumult,
Temples of need,
Trophies of hate.
Suffer it well.
Sacrifice all.
Remember, repentance,
See the knife,
Feel the knife,
Watch the knife fall.

Colour coding:
Green/orange,
White/black,
Blood red – all.

I had seen Paris before, dressed in a hundred garbs. She was a gaudy woman, tinsel spangled in the hair, bedecked in rubies, shining as the night-time vehicles displayed their red tail-lights in unending procession up the rising incline of the Champs-Elysées. She was an old lady, grand and elegant, too dignified to hurry through the historic palaces and stately buildings of her inheritance. She was a ghost of turmoil, simultaneously haunted and ennobled by her past centuries of chance and change. Enslaved in irons by history's dictates, she stood, a shackled pioneer, straddled between moods of democrat and adolescent, retaining the idiosyncracies of both and the perfection of neither. Rooted at the foot of the Eiffel Tower, the lady wore many layered garments of business and commerce, strangely unchanging through the centuries. A well-weathered madam and a city for all seasons – exciting to visit, difficult to love.

It was early Sunday morning when I drove towards her centre in some trepidation, remembering traffic of daunting proportions. I was in for a pleasant surprise. The route was uncluttered, the approach to the city was quiet, and the boulevards were almost deserted. It was very early and it was Sunday. Like a child with a new toy I drove round remembered places, not as a tourist, but as a pilgrim holding tryst with memories from past days.

Standing at the foot of the Eiffel Tower, in my

mind I saw myself carried by my father to the top and remembered the panoramic view. His strong hands had gripped my elbows tightly, as he balanced me safely to look over the edge of that terrifying drop. Today was Sunday so I did not visit inside on this occasion, but moved on to the Arc de Triomphe to enjoy a picnic breakfast on the Champs-Elysées. My memories were all there: the twin of London's Cleopatra's Needle, the Seine, Nôtre Dame, the artists on the pavement, and many, many, more sights to enjoy.

Arriving in Berne a few days later I found the Kursaal (the conference hall and centre) with relative ease. The week at the conference was most inspiring, with many new friends made. At its conclusion I was invited to stay at Bethany, a Deaconess Hospital and Community House in Zurich. The welcome from my fellow sisters was wonderful, and the building boasted a beautiful modern worship sanctuary and a quiet but creatively-designed garden. But best of all, the premises had a roof. Not just the kind that keeps the rain out – rather the kind you can walk on, sit on and meditate on with an incredible view of the city and the lake. Up there, for most of the day, I found the still point of my hectic, turning world again.

THE ROOF

What view calls Heaven into focus
And magnifies the grain of sand upon the palm?
From where shall earth become an orb again?
And holy shrines and habitats
Together cupped to catch the flood
Embrace all cares, all plans?

Moses-like, I'd mountain climb,
Or give the chase to David's flight,
Or gate-crash even lion's den,
Till, blinded on Damascus road,
I'd drop like Paul before my Lord
And see his face again.

So what is this, a humble roof?
Cement-mixed from beach-grain and water?
Its very flatness squaring every human sense,
To lock all thought-flight to the earth.
So who is this unchains the halter,
Undoing slip-knot, reef-knot, stake,
To let sail again the ship on Galilee?
And steps to me amid the storm,
God's feet, still wet from Jesus' walk upon the
    water,
And proves to humankind that all their frantic
    stir
Will one day end.

It was very hard to tear myself away from Bethany
where I felt so at home and at peace.

When I left Deaconesses Olga and Susan, I took
with me lasting memories of joy and true fellowship.
Then I drove down through Switzerland, passing
Interlaken, to the border.

There was something about the border-post
between Switzerland and Italy that I just could not
treat lightly. It was a small, unimpressive building at
that time. But arriving there marked a historic
moment for me. I pulled the car over to view it from
the other side of the road.

No one but me seemed to realise that, on this
particular day, a small border-hut had become a

landmark of achievement in the life of a little Irish leprechaun. I was here, at the door of Italy, at last. Tired, and hot, and eleven years late – but I had made it. All things were indeed possible to God.

I badly needed to celebrate. My heart was singing, my pulse was racing, and a combination of heat exhaustion, dehydration and adrenalin was playing havoc with my equilibrium. The man in the nearby shop looked up, startled, as I stumbled in the door, eyes shining, beaming from ear to ear. 'I'm celebrating,' I sang out, entirely forgetting what language he might speak. He grinned back, and in perfect English, asked me what I'd like. I rushed over to the fridge. 'Something cool,' I said. Well, what was the poor man to think? He reached for a can in the alcohol section. I laughed in glee and shook my head. 'No, no,' I grinned. 'There, this one.' His eyes followed my pointing finger to the huge, two-litre carton of cow's milk. His previously calm manner burst with an Italian exuberance which almost matched my own. He reached it to me and made no attempt to curb his ecstatic laughter as I pulled back the tag, put the huge carton to my head, and did not lower it from my lips until I had drained it to the cardboard.

'Thirsty,' I gulped! 'Irish,' he roared, 'Irish!' We stood laughing together while the shop rapidly filled with curious customers, each of whom caught the infectious atmosphere and joined in the joy. I stopped laughing fleetingly to catch my breath and looked round that tiny, homely establishment crammed now with hooting, friendly faces, not one of whom had the slightest idea what the joke was, or the long history behind it, and all nodding and patting my back and affirming my joy. They were just being there for me in my humanity and my need to rejoice. I whispered to the Master, 'Now this, this is celebrating!'

That night I stayed at Lake Lugano, and the next day, approaching Milan on the motorway, I began to be overwhelmed with prompting from the Boss. It came with that inner intensity which has no doubts. Knowing from experience how crazy it would be to ignore his leading, I pulled my car immediately off the road and prayed for direction. Since it appeared that I was not to continue southwards along that route, I turned eastwards – the only alternative exit at that point – and drove for a short distance until I could safely consult my map to see what lay along this new course.

Venice – the name called out to me from the creased map like a telegram from an old friend. I had always wanted to see it, but had not imagined that it would be on this trip since I had intended continuing south. It was one of those times when it is necessary to make a snap decision. 'Venice it is,' I said aloud, and pointed the car resolutely into the traffic again, abandoning all previous plans to put my motor on the train. It was to be one of the best decisions of my journey and, although I didn't know it at the time, it turned out to be the highlight of the trip for me. Even at this stage, I think, my heart suspected that it would be so. God never directs us towards second best.

Since Venice is a water-logged city and not too accessible for cars, I passed its turn-off sign on the motorway and searched instead the seaside town of Lido di Jesolo for lodgings. The morning was spent here on a shopping expedition for gifts to take home to the family. The day was punctuated with stops at the local ice-cream shops dining, and I do mean dining, on the kind of incredible Italian ice-cream which comes decked out with all the fancy trimmings and is a meal in itself. I am not, as a rule, a great fan of ice-cream, but when I saw my first one of these I couldn't quite decide if it was a Christmas tree bedecked early for Advent or a fantasy model of Disneyland. Either way, no main course was eaten that day.

The panoramic tour of Venice was booked for after lunch, or, in my case, post ice-cream. Picked up by coach at my pension, it felt good to leave my trusty steed to have a wee rest while I enjoyed the run to the port nearest Venice. From there the access to the city is by boat. It was a fairly difficult walk for me in the heat, to where the private craft ferried us across what our tour guide referred to as 'the Lagoon'. I couldn't help smiling each time she used that word, since my memories of childhood included the teasing I received every time it was mentioned that we would visit the River Lagon in Northern Ireland, because I would keep insisting that I wanted to see the lagoon.

Well, here I was, and here it was, and beautiful is too mild a description for it. The cool breezes on the water healed my exhaustion and travel-weariness, and the guide went out of her way to make sure that everything was as convenient as possible for me. On disembarkation the others went to see a glass factory, but all I wanted was to sit in the famous St Mark's Square and soak up the cosmopolitan atmosphere. I struggled the 200 yards in the boiling heat, 120 degrees in the shade, from the boat to the Square, with the perspiration running like a river from my forehead and into my eyes, almost completely blinding me so that I had great difficulty seeing my way forward. Over little bridges and past the famous Bridge of Sighs I stumbled, stopping frequently to mop my brow and wondering if the historical figures who had crossed that bridge to their execution had perspired less. Ah, well, at least I lived to tell the tale.

Safely arriving in St Mark's Square I sat for hours at the large pavement café making my glass of orange and piece of cake last through the little orchestra's entire recital. Bright sunshine, live music and the constant variety of nationalities parading before my eyes, produced a heady mix indeed. All around was the stimulation of life – the smell of freshly percolated coffee, the flapping of pigeon-wings as they dived and scavenged between the chair-legs and camera tripods. To my left an array of tourists as far as the eye could see; in front the grandeur and beauty of the Doge's Palace, and somewhere to the right I knew the gondolas slapped languidly upon the water on the rise and fall of the tide, riding at anchor in a forest of mooring-sticks.

By late afternoon I was able to move again, and strolled around the shaded cloisters where shops surround a large part of the Square, window-shopping only, due to the expensive price-tags. Slowly I made my way back past the Bridge of Sighs to the meeting-point with the rest of our tour. The sun was less burdensome now and I was looking forward to the gondola ride which some of us had booked.

Waiting for the others by the water's edge I was treated to the antics of the gondoliers. They were real characters, with extrovert and infectious personalities who delighted in playing to the crowd like market stall-holders. Dressed in traditional costume, their acrobatics on the moored boats and displays of wit with the waiting customers, made time pass quickly.

117

I lost count of the times they proposed marriage to me, balancing on one leg on the edge of the boat with a flower between the teeth. Fortunately for them I was laughing too much to venture a reply.

When we were allocated to gondolas, I was glad to be sharing with a family of four. The Perry family, with their boy and girl teenagers from Wales, have kept contact with me ever since. It was a boat-ride not to be forgotten.

The five of us filled the raft comfortably with the gondolier balanced on his feet behind. I had expected that this boat-ride would be different from anything I'd ever experienced before – but I never imagined the depth of peace and quietude of leaving the wide waterway to penetrate the smaller canals where motor-boats are not permitted. Tall, unbroken lines of tenement houses on either side seemed to snuggle in tight and rise so high that not a sound could squeeze through to shatter the imprisoned silence.

The serenity was awe-inspiring. Only the gondoliers themselves broke the mood, and that sparingly, when they needed to shout an instruction or greeting to a fellow colleague as he passed. Fleetingly, our 'captain' would treat us to a little music – not singing, but the most melodic whistling I have ever heard. Just little snatches offered spontaneously, and not for long. It felt as though he was happy in his work and it made us the more glad to be sailing with him. I lay back believing Venice could give me no greater thrill than what I had already received – but I was wrong. I had no idea what the hour would bring. The city had yet one more treasure to bestow. Upon the hour of six, every clock and bell struck out its peal. The very stones chimed in reverberation. Like a silver echo-chamber the narrow, enclosed waterways preserved and cradled the sound, enhancing and clarifying the tone and timbre, till I believed that my ears were being properly attuned for the first time. Nothing was harsh, all was soft and caressing, yet with such clarity and iridescence as to penetrate the very soul. This was Venice. It had shared with me its heart. I had found why poets came to this place. Venice taught me stillness, not removed from tension or trauma, but the contrast of God's incision into the heart of me. In the midst of the cacophony of this world's deafening jangle, we sometimes close our ears. We shut out the pain and in doing so we are robbed of the silence. For it comes not as bedlam's opposite, but as its contrasting companion. There is a relief in silence that is only felt after sound. There is a depth in joy that is appreciated only after sorrow. If we seek for peace we can find it in the midst of turmoil or we will never find it at all. Jesus said: 'I do not pray that thou shouldst take them out of the world, but, that thou shouldst keep them from the evil one.' (John 17:15)

FEASTS OF THE SENSES

Listen to Venice
Moored gondolas
Slapping aimlessly, methodically,
Upon the lagoon's surface,
Straining gently at the rise and fall of the water,
See the forest of mooring-sticks
Rise dank and protective,
Like a wetlands reedbed in the sun.

Move inland now from open water.
Hear the omnipotent silence
Caught with powerful acquiescence,
Incarnated between narrow channels,
As buildings rise tall, a double arm's stretch
   apart.
Holding all captive who traverse the pinched
   span
Of little man-made tributaries,
Capillaries to the heart.

High above my head legs dangle
From a window-ledge.
A flower, thrown by a child,
Down, down, to rest upon my foot,
Not the only eyes to watch my progress,
Many windows disguise a face.
Some watchers admire
The passing trade in tourist curiosity
But silence is the King.
The hour is struck
And peals of every tone and volume
Are released like doves.
Scrambled messages of winged breath to
   heart's cote.
The tall habitats around, now cocoons awash
   with bells,
Fill the senses till only the release in laughter,
Makes it possible to bear the joy,
And then is silence heard.
What before was soporific and placating,
Now becomes a spear of healing to the soul.
An incision so deep within my tension
That I am cleansed by its catharsis
And freed to enter depths of quietude
Undiscernible to the naked ear.

Lord,

Forgive me for the inclination to run and hide in the silence of whatever is my closet. I realise that this is not silence, but only the absence of listening.

Speak to me Jesus, in the bedlam; help me hear your still, small voice after the roar of the earthquake, wind and fire.

Please keep me listening through the turmoil, that I will not forfeit the healing touch of silence when it approaches, unexpectedly, at that same moment when my spiritual hearing is reverberating, uncontrollably, in pain. May I never be afraid to embrace its healing power, feel the refreshment, taste the joy. *Amen.*

Today my objective was to get to Rome; however, delayed by traffic snarl-ups I found myself, very late and in the dark, still on the motorway, praying fervently for help to find a night's lodgings. I turned off about 50 miles before Rome at an exit marked 'Orte'. Here I found a very small place, and not one which looked as though it held much promise as far as tourist accommodation was concerned.

I drove at a crawl around streets of row upon row of houses in the tiny settlement. Time slipped by as I crawled round yet another bend. The dark and the lateness lent its own sense of urgency to my fears. 'Please, Lord,' I prayed again, 'somewhere here must be a safe place to lay my head tonight. It doesn't have to be very wonderful, just clean.'

Again, I turned into the housing estate, scanning the darkness for any sign, any direction at all. It was completely deserted. At that late hour I knew I could not just knock at a door – besides, what about the language barrier? I swung my wheel slowly to round another bend and caught a glimpse of something on my peripheral vision. I slammed on my brakes as a small child scampered in front of my headlights and another followed after a runaway ball. They stood there, in night attire, grinning cheekily and waving a greeting. I jumped out and bent to speak to the youngest. 'Shouldn't you be in bed, love?' All I got was a grin. The older child was staring at me mesmerised and, before I could say a word, she took my hand and, in the natural, unquestioning way that children have, led me up the pathway to her front door.

The mother appeared in a high state of dudgeon. Ignoring me entirely, she released a torrent of Italian rhetoric at the two infants and dispatched them to bed as I stood quietly on the doorstep until it was accomplished. She returned to the threshold smiling sheepishly at me and whispering her thanks in one of the few phrases of Italian that I could understand. I tried to express that I had contributed very little to the scenario, apart from not running them down and, in a pause for breath, heard the lady reply in excellent English.

She was able to direct me to a hotel established mainly for long-distance lorry-driving clientele. I was puzzled at first because, in my repeated circling of the tiny hamlet, I had driven several times up and down the nearby street she was describing without seeing a building that looked anything like a hotel. But, when I drove back now I realised that it seemed to be just another square-blocked building surrounded by lorries, and not being able to read the signs, I would never have imagined it to be a hotel.

But hotel it was, and the outside did no justice whatsoever to the clean and even luxurious bedrooms inside. Once I had parked my car in the midst of the herd of articulated lorries, the lady proprietor led me to a beautifully-decorated room with an *en suite* bathroom and toilet and, wonder of wonders, air-conditioning. I was in heaven, and the price was very reasonable indeed. In fact it turned out to be the most suitable accommodation of the whole trip. So much so that I stayed there again on the way home – and what about the lorry drivers? Well, they treated me like the perfect gentlemen they were. I think it was a novelty for them to have a lady staying there. Their Italian chivalry rose to the fore and I was bought more glasses of orange juice than I could drink. There were lots of chats about Northern Ireland, and about my Boss – and the lady manager kept a motherly eye throughout.

Much witnessing to God was done that night and the following morning also, as most of them seemed to understand good English. I like to think I broke the monotony of the journey for them, as their good-natured conversation did for me. Only in heaven will I hear from the Boss the full extent of the subsequent influence of that night's witnessing.

Rome today – it doesn't sound like much when you write it down in a simple two-word phrase, but for me, it was a day for the history books.

I had arranged to meet a friend from the Berne Conference for breakfast at 7 a.m. in the YMCA. This Deaconess had a prearranged appointment at the Vatican and we had talked about seeing Rome together. However, I had not reckoned on the idiosyncratic nature of the traffic in the city centre. I had seen some metropolises on my travels through the years, doing battle with the city centres of Amsterdam,

Paris and Brussels, not to mention autoroutes and autobahns across the Continent. But my greatest driving challenge was when I took on the centre of Rome.

The first traffic light I arrived at brought me to a halt, chiefly because the light was showing red. All around horns of deafening volume honked and hooted and generally blew my mind. Small dark-haired men with tight curls and red faces shouted phrases I thankfully could not understand, but the tone was unmistakable. In horror my eyes checked the light again – it was still red. Then I realised what I had done wrong. I had stopped at a red light. On every side cars were blithely ignoring the lights and playing an anarchic game of dodgems which more resembled Russian roulette, to gain right of way against the contrary flow of traffic. It did not appear to matter whether a driver had a green or red light on their side: the object of the exercise appeared to be to continue the journey without having to stop and preferably without hitting anyone. I was to witness similar scenes many times that morning on my way to the YMCA.

When two opponents came close to collision or blocked each other's path, a verbal row, as big as a fight, ensued with each man climbing on the other car's bonnet and screaming as loudly as possible, perhaps to drown out the resulting cacophony of motor horns from the surrounding irate, and by then motionless, traffic. At one point, being at a standstill behind two such protagonists, I began to realise I would not reach the YMCA at the pre-arranged time. I was grateful to arrive at all exhausted and very late, but, thankfully in one piece

By now it was 8.45 a.m. and my friend was about

to leave, as she was shortly due to attend the audience at the Vatican and had no transport. There was only one thing to do: she and I both jumped back into my car and headed for that city within a city, where I never imagined I would tread. A special gentleman was about to receive a visit from not one, but two Deaconesses of the reformed faith. I am not sure how she had done it, but Olive had procured a second ticket to the huge chamber where he, whom the Italians affectionately call *Il Papa*, speaks to 1,000 or so folk, simultaneously, at a public audience. However, my main objective at that moment was to honour my promise to get my friend there safely. We were late, and by the time we had done battle with the one-way streets and the heat and the Italian eccentricities of traffic-light behaviour, we were extremely late indeed. By the time we arrived at the gate, it was so late that no one would allow me inside the walls to park my car.

But a promise is a promise; I had to keep going. Round and round the stout, impenetrable, walls of Vatican City we drove, from gate to gate, with every official reiterating the point that by now the audience must be half-finished and the door would not be opened to us at this stage in the proceedings. The heat was extreme, reducing my walking ability to a matter of yards. Yet I knew that God had led me here.

Just outside the walls I stopped driving for a few seconds of prayer, not knowing that I had halted, momentarily, in the public car park reserved only for coaches. My friend, as determined as I was, began talking with a coach driver. He heard me pray and pointed to the cross around his neck and the one around mine: 'Christian,' he said. It sounded less like a question and more an affirmation. I nodded enthusiastically and began to witness to him on the subject of the reformed tradition's scriptural understanding of repentance and commitment to Jesus as Saviour and Lord. He beckoned me to follow him to a very small space between his coach and the wall. It was such a tight space that it was incredible to imagine that my car might be able to squeeze into it, but it did. 'I will look after it for you,' the man said. 'It is my sacrifice to Jesus.'

Looking at my watch was now pointless: the only justification for continuing was obedience to God and trust. I was finding the going really tough, stumbling with exhaustion in the heat. Realising that Olive had suddenly left me, I looked round to see her step out in front of an approaching car which was heading for the main entrance. Its occupants, a mother and daughter who worked inside the walls, agreed to drive us through the gates and drop us off at the entrance to the audience chamber. Few words were spoken because of the language barrier, but I shall never forget the embrace we exchanged and what our eyes conveyed to each other as I alighted inside the walls.

There was still walking to do and the temperature would have blown a gasket on any gauge to which I was accustomed. On reaching the impressive entrance-door of the huge chamber, I was exhausted and dehydrated from the rigors of the day – without proper breakfast, not to mention without loo – and more than that, I was late, late beyond all conception of lateness.

The very tall guards on duty paid no attention whatsoever to what must have seemed to them like my innate babblings at the door. They kept their heads staring forwards, held high, their eyes almost unblinking, as I talked earnestly to the buckle on their waist-belts. The solid door was tight shut and bolted from the inside.

I cannot say how many minutes the four of us stood there, me talking non-stop, until there was an unexpected rasping sound from inside and someone must have glanced out at a level above my head, unobserved by me. The next thing I heard was the sound of bolts being pulled back across the inside of the door, which swung open in a wide arc to reveal a tall man in an extremely modern three-piece suit. I was taken aback, not because the door had opened – after all the Bible tells us we are to expect prayer to be answered – but because a three-piece suit is not what I had anticipated seeing at that precise moment. Perhaps I had imagined the building full of the bright red of cardinal's robes, or the purity of white – but steely grey and business pin-stripe? I was flabbergasted.

He was the epitome of Italian charm and quietly informed me of his position as one of the personal advisors to the important gentleman at the top. He listened most courteously to my story and, without question, told us to follow him. As we moved inside I asked him if the audience was almost over. His answer stunned me with another so-called coincidence. He explained how *Il Papa* had been leaving that morning to attend the audience when a most urgent telephone call from a head of state had called him back into his office, and it had been necessary to delay the starting time. In fact the matter was one of such importance that the huge crowd of people were still waiting for the proceedings to begin.

Inside the hall the sight was both awe-inspiring

and surprising to me. It was quite modern, and its bowl-like appearance accommodated the huge numbers easily; yet the almost circular shape produced an unexpected feeling of intimacy which I would never have imagined possible in the presence of such large numbers of people. I might have anticipated the singing, but nothing could have briefed me to expect the spontaneous myriad of voices. Every nationality and personality imaginable, were, without orchestration or direction, giving vent to their feelings of praise and rejoicing to God, each singing in their own language and without competition to the other. Spasmodically different groups struck up their own particular band of instruments, many of which were appropriate to their nationality. It all retained the heightened atmosphere of the circus and yet succeeded in maintaining the reverence of a cathedral. The air was alive with the exuberance of celebration, yet there was nothing irreverent or contrived about the worshippers, and all around people were quietly praying.

On entering this immense assembly I made an attempt to squeeze into the back row – an extremely Presbyterian trait in any gathering – and was immediately prevented from doing so by my three-piece suited friend.

'Come,' he said. 'Come forward.' Now I thought that perhaps he had spotted a seat a little further up the aisle which would be less crushed and uncomfortable, so I followed. Forward we proceeded, for one row, two rows, ten, twenty and he kept walking. On every side people reached out to greet me, with smiles of welcome and pats of encouragement. One old lady pressed her handkerchief into my hand, with tears running down her face pleading, 'Pray, pray, please pray for me. Tell him to pray for me.' I wondered where she thought I was going. I was looking for a seat. But the man in front was still walking.

By the time we were three-quarters way into the hall it began to dawn on me that he had no intention of stopping until he reached the front. He was obviously going somewhere specific. We had almost reached the stage now. There were a few spaces near the front, and the man signalled my friend into a seat there. Then he placed his hand beneath my elbow and steered me onward.

Above the noise of the audience's rejoicing I could hardly make myself heard. I attempted the question, 'Where are you taking me?' If I had moved forward a few paces I could have easily stretched out my hand and touched the central chair from which the audience would be addressed, positioned as it was in the centre of the low stage. He indicated for me to sit down here facing the stage and directly opposite the chair. To my right I observed that a couple of people were sitting in wheelchairs.

My guide bent over and whispered with deliberate definition and urgency of tone, 'When the speaking is ended, do not leave. Your day will not be finished.' I must have looked puzzled because he repeated, 'Stay in your seat. I will come to you; it will not be at an end.' Then he left me, my mind whirring, I dared not speculate, I just thanked God for his provision so far. Against all odds, he had led me here. I knew that the Lord was aware how adamantly I hold firm to the doctrine and faith of the reformed tradition, and he also knew what I long to communicate to those of a different tradition, especially as regards my homeland of Ireland. Whatever was about to happen, of this I was in no doubt: that my Saviour had guided me to this point for his purpose and had made it possible for my safe arrival and admission. All else was fully within his providence and I had to trust it to the will of God. My job was to obey my Father in Heaven.

Half-an-hour later, to the background of the racy drums of the Spaniards, and a pop-star welcome, in came the one whom that hot and passionate city calls *Il Papa*. Simply dressed in the distinctive white robe and skull-cap, his presence seemed unsophisticated in contrast to the pomp and colour of the flame-red cardinals who followed behind. The proceedings lasted about three-quarters of an hour. In addition to the various offerings of music and praise from the visiting groups from around the world, the sermon lasted roughly five minutes, but had to be repeated in at least seven languages, all of which he used with apparent ease and fluency. This fully occupied the remaining time of the audience.

He spoke directly concerning the nature and the person of Christ. During the time when the choir sang he fixed his eyes forward on my position, seated as I was directly in front of his chair. We held each other's gaze for a very long time, motionless, and then he slowly, and with deliberation, inclined his head downwards twice, in a repeated nodding action, without smiling. Needing no words of confirmation, I knew at that moment that we would speak together.

When the proceedings ended my three-piece friend was already at my side. There was a huge burst of activity as the audience surged forward to get a closer look. Some had even managed to push into the area where I had been seated. For a few seconds it was almost frightening, as I had no way of knowing how undisciplined the crowd might become. However, theirs was a restrained exuberance and my friend impressed upon me again that I should not leave. 'Here,' he said. 'Stand on the chair.' Up I climbed and was now head-and-shoulders above the crowd. Then the man whispered again in my ear, only just loud enough to be heard over the acclaim of the people, 'He will come first to the wheelchairs, then he will come to you.'

It was official now, we were to speak. It happened as the man had said it would. Inclining his head upwards to look into my face as I stood on the chair, that gracious statesman and head of his Church listened, and it was the depth and quality of his listening which impressed me most. The conversation was very short, but memorable, and his eyes throughout told me how he cared for Ireland and how he felt for our pain.

LIFESPAN

How wide the stretch of history's narrow bridge,
That spans the years and gives the lie to earth's
    pale distances,
And fathoms height and depth where fear and
    privilege hide
The destiny of God by sepulchre and robe
    entombed inside.
And all the earth conspire together
With true, sincere and pious zeal
To fight with code and law and creed,
To keep separate and to tear apart
Those whose common vision hides God's
    common heart.

And how quietly the Lord of all creation
With such subtlety and gentleness
Embroiders his vast tapestry of re-creation
Till all the threads of hate untangle,
Leaving naked love unclothed
And vulnerable before destiny, uncharted and
    unsought.
And how he touches soul of humankind,
Face to face, to tryst with mirrored truth,
Till eye to eye the Lord flays crossbar naked
And carries once again the wood to Calvary,
And shows to both his body hanging free.

I did not stay that night in Rome. By the time I
had battled for many more hours with the traffic, getting my friend to her train home, I was exhausted.
Besides, after the events at the Vatican, which of
Rome's mere tourist attractions could have super-
seded the experiences of the morning? I left the city
and headed to Naples hoping to find a b&b there.
Unfortunately the 'See Naples and die' adage almost
became a twisted reality for me, as I got lost in a
rather sleazy part of town and ended up in a resi-
dential ghetto of the city at dusk. It was a housing
estate of multi-storey flats where washing hung from
every aperture and dogs foraged on the scraps that a
woman threw out of a third-floor window as I
passed. My car roof received a sample of the offering
as I swerved to avoid a group of infants answering
the call of nature in the street. But it was the sight of
the little knots of young men bunched together on
every corner, playing casually with lethal-looking
flick-knives, that encouraged me not to delay my
departure. I drove on to Sorrento.

The next day I enjoyed a wonderful boat-ride to the Isle of Capri. Driving round the famous Amalfi Drive later that day was less relaxing, to say the least. Although in Ireland we understand about narrow roads, they are not usually traversed at the same speed as a motorway. But this was Italy and to make matters worse, the size of horn used unsparingly never seemed to correlate in any sense to the size of the vehicle. Driving along at normal speed, I would suddenly be blasted out of my skin by a mega-sized hooter, only to see in the mirror a car similar to Noddy's tootling alongside, shaving my paintwork as it rounded the next bend, overtaking me and driving onwards on the wrong side of the road. There seemed to be very few exceptions to this rule. No wonder, then, that the beauty of this scenic drive, spectacular as it was, somewhat escaped my aesthetic appreciation.

Winded in nerve and limb, I was glad to roost for the night in a little hotel in Positano. I say 'roost' because most of the accommodation in the neighbourhood seemed to cling for dear life to the cliff-face. As the picturesque hamlet was built on terraces, many of the buildings appeared to be part of the solid rock-face hanging by a thread at varied and varying levels above the sea. Mind you, the view was unparalleled and my time on the roof, before breakfast, was unforgettable. Oh to be a seagull now that summer's here.

Driving on, I turned northwards and by-passed Rome, stopping only for a brief lunch at the very foot of the live volcano, Mount Vesuvius, and a brief look at the ruins of Pompeii. The corpse forest of still parched and roasted ground surrounding the area bears testimony to the lasting scars of that devastation.

POMPEII

How shall our lives be
When we meet the Saviour,
Facing the Lord at the ending of time?
A quicksand of temperament, never
   remoulded?
A fire-eaten forest of conscience ignored?
Hard scabs of bitterness, hurts unforgiven,
Stench of the sulphur still on our clothes?

Or shall he sow new seed through ravaged
   corn-fields?
Shall healing come to the scorched, smoking
   ground?
When will we let him remould us completely?
Fleeing from lava flow, souls make no sound,
Remembering Lot's wife,
Keep faithful, keep trusting,
Don't turn around.

Having left the motorway to avoid the crippling
toll charges I drove northwards with a niggling anxiety about my fuel-levels in these seemingly empty
mountain roads. When the engine switched to the
reserve tank, I stopped the car at the side of the road
and told the Boss how worried I was. I think he
knew already, but it was good to talk. 'It has to be
soon Lord,' I pleaded. 'Where can I stay for the
night?'

There was nothing in sight but countryside and
hills. The stillness was interrupted only by bird-song
and insect noises. No inner prompting came whatsoever. I was devastated. 'What's wrong?' I cried. 'Why

am I not hearing you, Lord?' I had no choice but to keep going until the petrol, literally, ran out. I drove 100 yards or so, rounded a bend and there, straight in front of me was the most beautiful sight I think my eyes have ever welcomed. Large modern gates lay open to a meticulously-kept entrance and landscaped grounds leading down to a sparkling, man-made mountain lake, where folk were engaging in every water-sport imaginable. The legend on the entrance proclaimed it to be a camp-site open to all travellers. I cried with joy and apologised to the Boss. 'Sorry,' I wept. 'No wonder you didn't give me an urge to go anywhere. I had already arrived and didn't even know it.'

Here at Bolsena, somewhere between Rome and Florence, my frantic travelling came to a temporary halt and I spent a wonderful and restful weekend with the car as my bed once more. The management understood my predicament, stranded without cash because it was a Bank Holiday and fiesta, and with the utmost hospitality and kindness allowed me to postpone payment of the bill until the bank in the tiny local village down the road opened again on Monday.

The weather was glorious for my financially embarrassed and enforced rest. I was even gifted with the most gorgeous view from my 'bedroom' when the manager allocated me a site right down at the very edge of the lake. I was able to step straight out of the car onto the beach.

Erecting the curtains in the heat was never an easy task and I would start at 7 p.m. or sometimes even as early as 6 p.m. Then I would lie very still, in communion with the Boss, for hours while the light waned and the happy evening noises of the campers beyond my cocoon dimmed into the stillness of night.

The little children always found my car-bedroom a great source of amazement. I would hear the German *kinder* piping incredulously to their mothers in adjoining caravans and campers, 'Auto-slepin', Mama, Auto-slepin'?' Often they would gather round my camping-stove during my rather erratic meal-times and watch the antics as I struggled with the Kosangas gas-stove. When it finally gave up the ghost on my first day at Bolsena, I had to beg for hot water, and a cup of tea became the event of the day. I could have sold tickets to the infant audience when I was reduced to eating my final two eggs raw to avoid starvation. Their faces were a picture as I swallowed the eggs down in a gulp-and-a-half. Mind you, my own face, in the effort, wasn't exactly that of the Mona Lisa either. There was an extremely well-stocked supermarket on site but, as I couldn't afford to buy anything until Monday, I survived on those eggs and a packet of crisps for two days. It did wonders for my waistline but not for my rumbling tum.

As early as I could on Monday morning I was up and away to the local village and waited a long time for the bank to open. I then filled the car with petrol, returned to the camp-site to pay my bill, and gladly restocked my larder once more. As soon as I bade my neighbours farewell, I was off like the wind in the direction of home.

I came off the motorway at Pisa and cast an unsymmetrical eye over the leaning Tower. Approaching it across the grass, rocking at speed, as is my normal walking gait, there were times I was not quite sure which of us was the more askew, the tower or me. If

I can keep my balance as long as it has, I'll do alright.

By the evening I was on the Italian Riviera, and at Rapallo I searched for an overnight stay. Having tried several places, in desperation again I prayed, 'Show me, Lord, please show me which road to turn along.' Before Genova, within the cluster of the little villages of Camile and Recco, the roads were twisty and many were steep. All around me hamlets were built on layers rising above my head. I lifted my eyes upwards and there, on a steep hill above me, its neon sign brighter and clearer than any in the vicinity, was a small hotel which bore the name Hotel Elena. Immediately, in my mind's eye I saw the face of my Auntie Ellie. All my life this lady has been a real prayer giant, faithfully and continually remembering all my concerns, and my heart warmed inside me when I thought of her, perhaps even now, on her knees, before bed-time, praying for my safety – and here was Hotel Elena. My aunt's name was Ellen, but we called her Ellie. I knew, without a doubt, there would be room in that place for me. God had used the familiar to guide me amidst foreign surroundings.

When I eventually managed to reach the doorway I received a warm welcome from the staff, who did not seem to be at all concerned at being roused at that time of night. It did not surprise me when, at my request for a room, the manager reached behind to the key-rack and lifted down a fob which hung there in glorious isolation, handing it to me with the words, 'It's the last one, Miss; you are fortunate.' Believe me, I knew exactly just how very fortunate I was that night.

The next day I drove from the Italian to the French Riviera. I noticed immediately that the horns were softer in tone and abused less often. Continuing round the coast I crossed the border near Monte Carlo and found a camp-site in Cannes. It was very small and extremely inexpensive, less than £2 for a space. I could hardly believe my good fortune even though it was only a field with a glorified water-tap and basic essentials – and was very full.

It had been a claustrophobic night, curled roughly horizontal and clam-like on my driver's seat, squeezed between the car door and my case which I had wedged between seat and brake-lever to prevent me from rolling off my makeshift bed. I awoke at dawn and, as quietly as I could, engineered myself into a sitting position, pulled down the drapes from the car windows, prayed that the engine would start first time, and, still dressed in pyjamas and slippers, drove on to the open road and away from the overcrowded site.

There was no traffic at all at that time of the morning and I soon found toilets where I could wash and dress, but in all my preparations for the day, my chief concern was to be on the other side of Cannes before the commercial pulse of the city got going. In my naïvety I thought I had safely missed the night-life – but how wrong I was.

The map showed me the road out of town, and I had picked what I thought would be the scenic route by the sea – but what was not indicated on the map was the fact that I was about to drive the length of the main promenade, along which are situated most of the night-clubs, casinos and general all-night rave spots of one of the most notorious gambling venues in Europe. Unknown to me these establishments close down at the time when the birds begin singing – just about the same moment as I turned my car into the long stretch of promenade to get to the other side of town. The narrow strip of an excuse for a beach ran the full length of the grand circular sweep of the promenade, stretched to its limits like an overextended rubber-band. It wasn't the only thing in that pitiably rich city that felt taut and used.

It came as quite a shock, after the self-imposed isolation of the cramped site where I had not spoken to anyone, suddenly to find that doors were being flung open the full length of the promenade and dozens, soon hundreds, of folk were pouring onto the street and literally mobbing the car. At first mine was the only vehicle in sight and some of the people thought it was a taxi. Quickly I checked that the doors were locked and tried to edge forward at a snail's pace. Progress was slow and, for the most part, non-existent.

I had ample opportunity to observe my uninvited companions at close quarters. There were men and women of all ages. I was surprised to see so many of the older generation, and I wondered why I was surprised. Perhaps I had assumed that the fashionable night-life of Cannes was mainly the prerogative of the young.

But these faces staring at me through the windows, stumbling, tripping, muttering under their breath as they staggered against the now almost stationary car, were slow faces with tired expressions. Some were obviously the worse for drink, but many were just tired. I did not see any eyes that shone. No figure came running from a building with head lifted high, rejoicing.

A tall man with grey hair was taking small steps towards the sea. He was most certainly a senior citizen, and in his hand he carried a flimsy paper bag of the variety collected from supermarkets to carry the weekly shopping home. There was no footpath on the seaward side of the car. The tarmac of the road merged, without definition, into the beach. As he stumbled, without direction, onto the sand, the breeze caught the bag and I could see clearly that it was empty. Despite a smart suit his tie was missing, and his shirt unkempt. It had obviously been a hard night. I could see by his stance and sluggish movements that he was dejected. I prayed for his safety as I drove slowly beside him, keeping watch on his progress. I could see that he was crying. Several times he looked inside the paper bag. Several times it showed empty.

What was he looking for? What had he lost? What had he hoped to gain? I thought of my Dad always coming home with something for me. Wherever he was, working away or at home, there would always have been something brought back in a paper bag for me. Monetary value was not the issue. I was thrilled with a shell or a leaf, or most special of all a feather from the beach with a picture of the bird that had moulted it, sketched by his own hand during his lunch-break. Sometimes he found a real treasure, a piece of driftwood or flint, and we would discuss together what we could see in the shape before his creative hands got to work to set the image free by carving or sculpting.

I wanted to help that bemused crowd in Cannes. I longed to show that tired old man the riches at his feet, on the beach, in the sea. Treasures that could not be gambled, those treasures that are beyond price. I prayed for the old paper-bag carrier and was glad when he headed safely for the bus stop – but every building I passed now seemed to rattle and twitch with tasteless light-bulbs and cheap glitter. I felt its emptiness, its disappointed hopes, its unfulfilled promises – and I just wanted to get away from there, to be free of the sleaze and the deception of the vain promises forced on those with hurts not healed, and self-esteem perverted.

As I broke free of the last of the stragglers, I raced to the end of the promenade and turned sharply round a bend which took me beyond sight of the long stretch of night-spots, their lights already growing dim in the slowly brightening promise of the rising sun. I found that I was gently sobbing. Without going inside one building, the dejection and frustration of those places had reached out and sullied my peace. I knew that I wanted none of it. I prayed through the tears, 'Lord, I don't want any of this. None of it. Not gold, not diamonds, if this is the feeling that attends such things then I want none of it. I want only what you have to give me. Lord,' I prayed, 'give me what you decide.'

At the precise moment when I finished my garbled, stumbled prayer, I turned another bend in the road and there was a lay-by on the seaward side, elevated a little above the road. I drove straight into it without pausing. The automatic car had hardly time to change gear as I turned off the engine and sprang out as fast as I could. Instantly, with the perfect timing that I have discovered God uses again and again, the sun, like a cork from a champagne bottle, burst above the horizon and spread a carpet of diamonds to my feet. Narrow was the spread and specific, shining as it did on each wave-crest individually, in a manner I had never observed before

nor, indeed, since. These diamonds were placed
meticulously and polished personally by a loving
Father who knew exactly what I needed and knew
how to be the provider.

DIAMONDS IN THE SEA

Sights I've seen and wonders,
Continents
    that it takes a whole
    month to drive across,
If you go real fast
    and don't heed
    the brutal rain
    in your face.
Those vast acres in memory's eye
    are small enough
    for a Daddy to carry home
    in a paper bag
To a waiting child.

But cracks in pavements –
    now there's a giant thing.
    No bigger than for a toe
    To catch on.
Yet I've been to toe-cracks big enough
    To lose a heart in.
And nothing comes bigger than that,
    except, perhaps,
    DIAMONDS –
Diamonds in the sea.

Father,
    Your surprises are the best. Flapping plastic
with supermarket handles could never contain

142

what you have in store for me. I have what I
need, thanks to you. Those diamonds were your
best idea yet. I cried with such joy when I saw
them. Thank you Father.

Show me how to wear them in the secret
recesses of my soul. God grant me taste in cloth-
ing myself spiritually that the tacky festoonments
of earth's greed may never render my form tasteless and vapid in your sight. *Amen.*

Driving on to St Tropez, that beach playground of
the rich, I was curious to see what it looked like from
all the legends I had heard. I found it to be only
almost as pretty as Ireland, except it bathed more
luxuriously in sunshine and wore an expensive price-
tag. I stayed a mere half-an-hour, long enough to take
a photograph and say a prayer of thankfulness to be
going home.

I journeyed northwards for the rest of the day
along the main artery of France. At one point it was
uncanny the way the sun seemed to stop suddenly on
the road where the car crossed an invisible line, the
other side of which was rain. It was very strange,
almost like going through a door. From then on the
greyness and dullness increased, and I realised that
I had, unknowingly, bidden farewell to the Continental sunshine. But I did not mind; I was going
home.

My objective for the day was to find Taizé, the
famous Christian community which I had heard so
much about during my studies at St Colm's College.
Nearly 3,000 young people were staying in tents that
week, but I was welcomed and allocated a bed in the
house for guests which was only available to me
because someone else had not turned up. I thanked

God for this additional answer to prayer. Again he met my need even before I knew the need was there.

The day was hot, wet and humid, but by this time in my long trek, I was so hungry for Christian companionship that I hardly noticed the weather. The campers had come from all over the world and for two nights I enjoyed the fellowship.

Although these few days represented an experience I would not have missed, I needed to get on the road again. Certain very practical emergencies were pressing me forward. For one thing I had, by now, gone through six pairs of shoes, three weeks being the maximum life-span of my footwear under normal conditions, and conditions on this trip could hardly have been described as normal. Once the stiffener in my left shoe has weakened from pressure of walking over on one side, the pair can only be relegated to the bin, no matter how unworn the right shoe may be, because there is simply not enough support left. The remaining shoes in my luggage all had nails sticking through from over-use, and I was depending on a combination of weak, makeshift cardboard stiffeners and strong hope. My feet were in ribbons, and everything I did not need to wear had been torn up in strips to use for bandages to protect my damaged toes. I was in a considerable amount of pain and had not been able to find a shop anywhere on my travels which sold the kind of shoes suitable for my feet.

The second consideration was less worthy – but none the less urgent. The local wasps were giants, and becoming so numerous as they swarmed around the plastic bowls of steaming hot chocolate which were served in the open air for breakfast each morning that, at times, I could hardly see my fellow breakfasters through the cloud.

144

I was eager to smell the English Channel and to dwell again within the sway of a sea that tangs. Reaching Caen before nightfall, I followed a couple who kindly led me to a camp-site which cost less than £1 – the cheapest yet.

The next day I drove the last lap to Cherbourg, joyously blowing my horn to greet the docks as I sped to the edge of the quay, and jumped out of the car to breathe deeply the familiar fishy aroma mingled with engine-grease. The feeling of 'mission accomplished' was strong in me as I daydreamed about being home again, remembering Daddy's words to Mum at the time of my first escapade to the Continent: 'You've got to lose your children to keep them, Betty.' He knew what he was talking about.

There was still much of the world I hoped to see, but driving past the familiar sights of Belfast I felt a touch of sentiment unknown before, realising that there was a great deal to be said for life in Northern Ireland, after all. Even the huge shipyard cranes called Samson and Goliath began to look less unwieldy in the evening sunset. These wingless cranes will never fly to foreign climes, I thought, but they too have their story to tell.

THE CRANES

You'll never fly –
Samson and Goliath,
Your stiff, arthritic limbs,
Crossbowed against the skyline.
Set in density of history,
Moulded from the foundry,
Of flag and chasuble and cross.
Crane by name and crane by nature,
But you'll never fly to nest on other shores.
Yet yours is the yellow blazoned light
That tells me I am home,
That navigates my way through braggart
current,
Your bludgeoning, blundering, solidness.
Planted in the dockland mud,
Standing staunch enough to make it firm,
As though a diamond cut your shapes
And rooted them in concrete blocks of love.
Imperfect crosses that you lift to heaven,
Piece on piece rough-hewn against the sky.
Registering flight's end, backlogged in
unforgiveness.
Archive to propensity, your welcome
embracing all my parts.
Unheeding of their sum, hungry only for
my blithe return.
Waiting at the doorway like my mother
To embrace, enfold and pray I'll never
go again.

8 A PILGRIM'S PROGRESS

The Holy Land: Jerusalem – Jericho –
Nazareth – Qumran and the Dead Sea –
Galilee

Some people are tourists. I have always preferred to
think of myself as a traveller – but this time, I was a
pilgrim.

They had all warned me before I went. 'It won't be
what you expect. Prepare to be disappointed. It's
nothing like the Biblical image of Palestine.' My
friends had prepared me well to see how the modern
world and the passing of time had transformed the
Holy Land into something less than biblical. I went,
but not to discover Jesus for he travelled with me,
and I hoped he would show me a little of his homeland. This he did.

The airport at Tel Aviv was modern and bustling
and could have been almost anywhere in the world.
It was only when the coach transported our holiday
party out of the airport and into the countryside,
heading for Jerusalem, that I began to realise that I
was in the Middle East. My first impressions were of
tremendous heat and field upon field of sunflowers.

In time we started to rise and I saw it, Jerusalem,
on the hills ahead. Like a bolt it struck me – we were
going up to Jerusalem. How many times I had read
that phrase in scripture, and only now realised that
when Jesus is described as going 'up to Jerusalem',

the gospel-writers were not making some abstract allusion to a capital city's superiority but rather he was, quite literally, climbing steadily as he journeyed onward because the city is built on hills. It was such a simple, yet illuminating discovery for me that I realised this wonderful land had much to teach the pilgrim.

It was fortunate indeed that our leader on this pilgrimage was a minister who had previously lived and worked in the Holy Land, and he kindly allowed me to choose an itinerary which would both be possible physically and also would allow me to avoid rushing from shrine to shrine. Instead I was keen to see mainly natural elements of the land which would have changed little from Jesus' day in preference to the man-made trappings of religion or local tourist board.

Our hotel overlooked the walls of the old city, and every morning at dawn I was awakened by the raucous chanting from a neighbouring minaret calling the faithful to prayer. Since it never failed to waken me, I decided the Lord might want my time employed in the same manner. So, each morning, before even the birds were up, I prayed silently at my window with the Dome of the Rock clearly visible across the narrow valley. The fragile tips of rising sun defined prisms of crystal in the profusion of scatterings of light along the skyline of a thousand spires and domes, and the Lord stayed by my side.

The day we visited Jericho I was looking for a tree. There were hundreds. This I had expected, but I wanted to find one, any one would do, but one placed in a strategic position on the road from Jerusalem, where a small man might climb to get a better view of the crowd and the approaching Messiah. I knew I would recognise it when I saw it – and I did. It was a sycamore, and it certainly looked close on 2,000 years old, and that was good enough for me.

After lunch, when the others were sightseeing, I came and sat in its shade and pressed my ear to its bark and ran my fingers through its leaves and found a low branch where a little man, about my height, could just reach to pull himself up into its canopy of leaves. For a short time I was Zacchaeus, desperately scrambling to the top to overlook the road and catch a glimpse of the famous teacher passing by.

ZAC'S CHAT

Never mind the vertigo,
They say he's something special,
I really don't know why.
But there's talk of miracles and wisdom
And water into wine.
Now there's a man who'd grace my table
If he ever came to dine.
I'd be something special
If I could land that fish.
It would be the party of the year,
Voted most prodigious.
No longer brunt of gibe and joke,
Nor ostracised for being me,
I'd be something special,
If the rabbi came to tea.
If this scum stopped throwing stones
I could get a better hold.

Then I'd have more authority
To be both dignified and bold.
When I call his name across this throng
He's bound to see my rich apparel
And know I don't belong
With such a rabble of a crowd
But have only climbed this tree
To be seen and to be heard.

Shush, here he comes now,
Well, he doesn't look so great.
You'd think he'd wear a decent robe and
Did he touch that leper? – wait!
He's moving to the bottom of the tree,
Yes, yes I think he's stopping,
He's going to speak with me.

What happened then Zacchaeus?
What exactly did you see,
From your vantage point of leaves,
Before the rabbi came to tea?
How did his eyes burn deeply to the axle
    of your soul?
Did he release in touch of wonder
All that made you whole?
Did he salvage from your conscience
God's image from your birth?
Did he joke about tree-climbing
To break your pride with mirth?
'Come down,' he said with clarity,
'I'm coming home for tea,'
I wonder at what point he said, 'Come,
    follow me.'

And you, a broken man, gave back a
　　hundred-fold, and more
Of all that you had stolen, to the people
　　you had fooled.
In poverty of spirit, now set free,
All because a Saviour paused below a tree.

Nazareth was always a market-place and it still is,
bustling and dusty with the meeting of a thousand
cultures, big business and commerce brushing shoul-
ders, unself-consciously, with small urchins herding
goats through the streets to sell.

I gave the local shrines and museums a miss, and
stationed myself instead in an open shop-front in a
busy side-street. Explaining to the proprietor that I
just wanted to watch the world go by, I felt relieved
when he did not need me to justify the request. He
nodded understandingly and brought me a chair.
Watching the world go by was a major occupation
thereabouts, and I was not alone.

Old men had perfected the art, chewing, drinking, spitting their way through the morning with a
dignified disrespect for Greenwich Mean Time and
twentieth-century deadlines. The only recurring in-
terval to mark the passing day appeared to be siesta
time, and that was a movable feast which seemed to
be applicable in any portion of the day and, in some
cases, appeared to be interminable. Yet all around,
business transactions were negotiated with contradic-
tory languidness and loudness, and the whole earth
seemed to revolve slowly without need of timepieces.

The fast feet were the children's, dodging, dipping,
ducking the huge trays of uncovered food carried
shoulder-high on the palm of a single hand and

sometimes balanced on the head. Occasionally an urchin would yelp unconvincingly as he dodged a kick or clout from a carrier who had almost tripped over their antics.

The animals were the greatest novelty to me. They were all there – sheep, goats, horses, camels, dogs, you name it – mixing easily with bearded Orthodox men, and veiled ladies, and three-piece-suited gentlemen with neat, expensive computers in tiny briefcases. The incongruity of a man sitting on a donkey, engrossed in his conversation on a mobile phone, was almost too much for my sense of culture-shock. I caught his eye and we both laughed. I wonder why?

SCHOOL-DAYS

Were your school-days happy, Lord,
Cocooned within this bustling brood?
Of panniers, and marketers, and words too rude
For Mary's gentle ears and Joseph's discipline?
And did you sit and listen as folk haggled over
     price,
And boys shouted obscenities
At the donkeys carrying lice?
And saw dogs kicked in market square.
While prisoners' eyes stared dead,
As the crowd assembled for a stoning,
To clear the business from their head?
And did you take your local penny
To buy the daily loaf,
Slowly bringing home the shopping
That Mary's family would be fed?
And was there time to stop awhile,
At the wood-smith's timber yard,
Delivering lists from father

Of the soft wood and the hard,
To be ordered for that table
Cousin Zac would need,
When young John had grown
And there'd be an audience to feed?
And the chair for Liz when her son had left
  her side,
And she, alone in the darkness,
Would sit quietly, and cry?
Would you carve a plaque then
In remembrance of that faithful prophet-child?
And would there be a long plank,
And a cross-bar short and wide
To support the hanging body,
Of another holy child?

On the way to the Dead Sea the bus drove through dramatic scenery. Red, craggy wilderness of rock and cliff overshadowed the road for most of the journey, and my biblical memories had at last encountered scenery within which to root my imagination. Here the pulsating, twentieth-century engine of the coach and the good road-surface were the only things to lend incongruity to the sensation of having been transported back into biblical times.

As we rounded a bend in the road, I was gazing upwards at the sharp cliffs and boulders that might have hidden any number of waiting marauders in Jesus' day, not to mention the Amalekites of the Old Testament era. When the bird bore down on us out of the sun, its huge, stretched, wingspan overshadowed the front of the bus, and for a second I remembered a previous experience in Glencoe, in Scotland. Thankfully, this time I was in a more durable vehicle. The passengers gasped in awe and showered the driver with queries. Was it an eagle, they asked? He nodded his head and kept driving. Yes, I thought, this was the scenery that could well support an Old Testament battle or two.

Sadly, even in modern times, war was in the air with jets overhead buzzing the sun-bathers as they stretched out on the sand surrounding the Dead Sea. The high density of salt in the water makes it possible for everyone to float. What a weird sight that was, to watch all shapes and sizes, creeds and cultures lying, motionless, face to sky, like beached whales, on the top of the water, as the low-flying jets buzzed them from above. It would have been interesting to hear the Lord's comments on it all.

RUMOUR ON!

'Wars and rumours of wars',
That's what he warned,
Never would the earth see peace
Until the Prince returned again.
Rumour on,
And set the teeth a-chattering,
Broken world,
And broken humankind,
Until the end of time.
But He had come,
To heal those great divides
For man and he,
And man and she,
And He and I,
What would my Lord command,
Expect of me?
To tell Son worshippers
Afloat upon the deadness of the sea.

Salt, my children,
That's why you're sent to earth,
Make it impossible for hope to drown,
Show the meaning of your second birth,
Salt, preservative of food for hungry souls,
Preserve my truth in every way you live.
Prepare the way to see your Lord
Descend again with sceptre in his hand,
Can you obey my great command?
To neighbour seek in trench of enemy,
Fight each smallest tyranny,
Till from the slavery of hate,
We see the earth set free.

Rumour on,
Tell far and wide the tale.
That since the Prince has died to conquer sin,
His risen Lordship of our lives
Will change the earth, as water changes rock,
And grain on grain, through countless centuries,
Prove by pain, that never will we be alone,
And never will His promise fail.

From there we travelled to Qumran itself. It had
been a full day's trip to discover again the cavern
where a small boy had found the famous scrolls
while herding his animals among the cave-pocked
cliffs.

The story goes that one of his sheep or goats had
wandered into the cave and he, in an attempt to
chase it out, had thrown a stone deep into its interior.
I expect he was trying to save himself what would be
a hefty climb, as the cave is high in the cliff-face and
none too accessible. However, when the stone produced a resonating clink, the boy's curiosity got the

better of him and he clambered into the dark interior to discover a number of earthenware jars containing the scrolls. The find was priceless in terms of what it revealed about ancient times and the meanings of much of the original language of the Bible in terms of everyday usage, thus throwing fresh light on scriptural allusions and phrases. During my theological studies I had chosen this subject for one of my theses and now, in the Holy Land itself, I was thrilled to see, at first hand, the cave and also the site of the early community of Essenes.

SHEPHERD'S TREASURE

They brought great gifts to manger-side
Two thousand years ago,
Straw-knelt and herded like humble sheep
    into the stable,
Treading without self-consciousness,
Where kings would also stoop.
Telling Mary of the angel choir,
And handing unblemished lambs
Into Joseph's unassuming arms.
Was goats-milk the wine that assuaged
    their thirst?
Shepherds, the angel's choice to visit stable?
To witness God's true glory now revealed,
Incarnate truth, forever more in earthen
    jars concealed.

To move from Jerusalem to Galilee was, for me, a move to paradise because of the blessed drop in temperature and because of the water. Fortunately it was a small beach, more pebbles than sand, but with shells that gleamed with the sheen of burnished pearl and the water lapping over them almost to the top of the steps, so that when I stepped through the gateway in the walled garden of my hotel, I was stepping almost immediately into the sea. It was a most glorious feeling, after days of swollen ankles and bloated feet, to tear off my stockings and plunge my aching toes into the iced coolness of Galilee.

The hotel in Galilee where we were staying was lovely. In the garden was a small one-storey apartment which I was allocated for the duration. My memories of the nights at Galilee were punctuated by the sweet smell of jasmine each night, as I walked through the garden to bed. I stopped at the apartment's front door to chat with the dozens of tiny lizards which ran up and down the lintel and across the handle, to perch on my arm and eat my scraps of leftovers from the day's packed lunch. They became real chums while I was in Galilee, and I really missed them when I left. I had to be careful, though, moving in and out of the flat, not to let them scurry through the door, as they seemed quite attracted to the warmth of my bed.

Of all the memories gifted to me by Israel's strange sights, sounds and smells, the most vivid come from the old city of Jerusalem itself.

Here, in the market-place, children were fleet of foot and quick of hand. As I stumbled along the Via Dolorosa, there were more small hands in and out of the tourists' pockets than I'd seen rabbits in and out of burrows. They bobbed, they ducked, they stood grinning from ear to ear as they neatly pick-pocketed their way from top to toe.

The walking was not easy in parts, as it was rough underfoot. At one point there was talk of hiring a donkey for me to ride. When the small boy arrived with the beast, apologising that his uncle, its owner, could not be there with it, I asked why and the reply was, 'He is ill in hospital with the bites from the fleas on the donkey.' Somehow I lost my enthusiasm for this particular mode of transport and continued to hoof it instead.

At the gates of the old city I asked to sit alone again for a while, to take in the moving cavalcade of ancient and modern as the locals pushed, prodded and drove their merchandise to market. One woman staggered up the steps towards me, wearing traditional dress, and balancing a huge burden on her head. It was too good a shot to miss and I reached for my camera. The reaction this produced was a great shock to me. Instantly she flung her burden to the ground and came at me like a tornado, brandishing her stick above her head and bearing down on me with screams and such a fluency of phrases that, if I had been aware of their translation, I would surely have known just how cursed I was.

Throwing my camera to the ground at her feet, I begged her forgiveness in non-verbal language known the world over. She stood frozen to the spot, staring at the camera where it lay as though she was unsure whether to stamp on it or run in the opposite direction. Even though she was veiled, I could discern the terror in her eyes. I remembered then how some races still view cameras with intense superstition, fearing that a person who captures their image in some way owns or has power over them, for good or evil. The lady was shaking now, and I deeply regretted giving her pain. I had had no idea that such an ancient superstition still existed in this modern, bustling city. It taught me again how old and new dwelt cheek-by-jowl in twentieth-century Jerusalem. I assumed the attitude of prayer and, aloud, begged both the lady and God for forgiveness, hoping she would understand my penitence and my genuine concern for her health. She calmed a little and stopped shouting, but gave both the camera and myself a wide berth as she reinstated her burden on her head and moved onward. I prayed a long time for that lady and her family.

In the old city, at another place, there was a very cramped and narrow gate in the walls where merchants used to pass through to market. I visited this door, and imagined Jesus sitting as a boy laughing with the other children to see fat, wealthy merchants attempting to push exhausted camels, bearing huge and overloaded panniers on their flanks, through this narrow aperture. What a hilarious sight it must have been to watch these greedy businessmen shove and push, heave and tussle, with their noisy beasts. Businessmen who preferred to endure the indignities of red faces and bruises rather than relieve the animal of even the slightest portion of its cargo, that the last drop of profit might be milked that day at the market-place.

How many, I wonder, had Jesus witnessed getting stuck, quite literally, in that gate known to the locals as 'the eye of the needle', with their produce spilt wastefully upon the ground? What a wonderful visual aid it presented him, when, grown as a man, and teaching the people, he used the visual memory available to his listeners as a dramatic teaching-tool when he taught that, 'It is easier for a camel to go through the eye of a needle than for a rich man to enter the Kingdom of God' (Matt. 19.24). How the audience must have laughed, sharing Jesus' sense of humour, as they recalled the familiar picture in their minds. Immediately his message would have struck home even as the laughter died – humour and drama were two of the best channels that Jesus used to communicate his wonderful truths. As a Christian dramatist, sitting watching the world go by in the streets of Jerusalem, I received God-given inspiration for a lifetime.

But the most enduring memory of all was the one afforded me at the Garden Tomb in Jerusalem. It was here that I received what was for me the definitive experience of my pilgrimage.

The group had already visited this garden on the previous day and I returned the following day to spend time quietly, where two large crevices in the rock make holes like eyes in the cliff-face known as The Skull. Below this reputed site of Golgotha, the garden nestles at the foot of the cliff. It is an area kept simply, without shrine or edifice, boasting merely a natural cave which is said to be the tomb where they laid my Master after his crucifixion and death.

I desperately wished to be by myself in that cave. To stand quietly with my private thoughts, sharing with the Master, alone. But the Lord had other ideas, for he is in the business of growth and making disciples. Another man, a fellow tourist, visited the cave with me. As I entered through the doorway, which was a simple wooden plank, I saw only a low, natural rectangular ledge of earth and rock, built to one side of the cave, where a body might be placed. Nothing else occupied that cavern and, as I turned to view the inside of the door, I saw a sign which read, 'He is not here, he is risen.'

As I read the sign, I felt the presence of the Lord, not in the tomb, but within me. The fellow traveller in the cave also seemed to experience it for himself. For the first time in my life, I did not need to be alone: I was honoured to share the joy of this moment with a fellow pilgrim. It was as though the presence of Jesus pre-empted all other priorities of need or circumstance, as though his nearness blocked out all consideration of anything but himself, and with him in control all creatures became one and a spiritual sharing was possible. The two humans in that space stood, without needing to speak, a distance apart, yet somehow for a few moments, by God's touch, we were one in our experience of Christ. I knew then that human greed of individuality could have no place where the Master had chosen to break the bonds of death. He was risen! Here was joy.

JOY

I've seen the seekers of joy
Pursuing happiness
Across the fault-lines of the earth.
Some in wild and careless pleasure,
A closing of the palm upon the beach
To make a fist of sand,
And long before the fingers open,
Tell-tale signs of granules draining,
Oozing through the knuckles,
Predict an empty hand.

The world is small to circumvent,
To feel God's breath upon my soul
Discovering his life in me and joy –
It is a harvest word,
Not garnered from half-grown seeds,
But ripened by the heat of suffering
Peace comes, as silence follows rain.
Christ met me in the tomb
And there I lived his truth again,
'He is not here, he is risen.'